What Ails Library Websites of Research and Technical Institutions of India

WHAT AILS LIBRARY WEBSITES OF RESEARCH AND TECHNICAL INSTITUTIONS OF INDIA

Shalini Wasan
PhD, Library and Information Science
Senior Librarian, Chandigarh College of Engg. & Tech
(CCET Degree Wing), Chandigarh

Ess Ess Publications
New Delhi

WHAT AILS LIBRARY WEBSITES OF RESEARCH AND TECHNICAL INSTITUTIONS OF INDIA

ISBN : 978-93-87698-26-0

First Published 2019

Published by:
Ess Ess Publications
4831/24, Ansari Road,
Darya Ganj,
New Delhi-110 002.
INDIA
Phones: 23260807, 41563444
Fax: 41563334
E-mail: info@essessreference.com
www.essessreference.com

Cover Design by *Patch Creative Unit*

Printed and bound in India

Dedicated to
Book Lovers all Over the World
with the Grace of
Almighty Goddess
Maa Sheetla

Contents

Acknowledgements

I thank the Almighty God for his multitude of blessings that enabled me to complete the work on this book well in time. I would like to express my gratitude to Jessica Chambers from Sitebeam for facilitating the access of Sitebeam Web Analyzer. I would also like to thank Dr. Akhandanand Shukla for his guidance and support. I would also like to thank Mr. Aman Narang for helping me during my work period. I take this opportunity to express my immense gratitude and admiration to my parents Mr. A. P. Wasan and Mrs. Navneet Wasan. My heartfelt thanks goes to my brother, Anurag Wasan and sister-in-law, Mrs. Pooja Wasan who have been very patient and supportive during the entire course of time involved in preparing this book. My daughter, Purvi Wasan and two sweet nieces, Aahana Wasan and Adiva Wasan earn my unmitigated gratitude for their love and affection while being a constant source of inspiration and energy throughout my work.

— **Author**

Preface

The world is presently experiencing tremendous information overload which needs to be communicated in an appropriate and desired manner to information seekers. Information Communication Technology (ICT) is playing a vital role in promoting the interaction and interplay of information among populations. The impact of ICT can be seen in every sphere of life. The World Wide Web has become a popular communication tool of choice for accessing and sharing information on the internet. The most convenient way for dissemination and communication of broad based information is through websites. The library website has undergone dynamic change both in the means of communicating with the users and the nature of the service itself because of the use of and by bringing in new extensions of professional tools used by librarians worldwide. It is a digital gateway to library services and resources. A well equipped and updated library website should provide online information about traditional library collections and services, provide access to online resources, perform information services online, guide and educate users, communicate space management for library users (for feedback and lodging complaints) while simultaneously promoting the library and its website. The library website is the primary source of information for its users. The most important part of any website is that it should have the latest updated information which is easily accessible. Many institutions have developed library websites in order to provide information regarding various institutional facilities, resources and services offered to users for fulfilling their information requirements. The above line of thought exposes the fact that current library websites are an absolute necessity. Webometric tools and techniques are required to assess websites. This book is presented in five chapters. The first introduces the website layout and its basic structure. The second deals with Webometrics Perspectives and the third deals with Webometric Techniques. The fourth chapter deals with the Quantitative and Qualitative Assessment of Library Websites. The fifth and last chapter deals with the Implications of Library Website Assessment.

This book is useful for students, teachers and research scholars as well as professionals of Library & Information Science. The book presents the challenges, strengths, opportunities and limitations of library websites. It serves as an indispensible guideline for Librarians and Webmasters to aid the evaluation process of their library websites that is inclusive of futuristic design as well as content management.

— **Shalini Wasan**

1

Website Layout: Basic Structure

1.1. INTRODUCTION

It is extremely easy to access all forms of information on almost any topic on the Internet today. However, whether or not that information is reliable, up-to-date and unbiased is a moot question for anyone conducting research on the web. It is essential, therefore, to ascertain the authenticity of the website from where information is being garnered. The basic criteria for evaluating a website include - Accuracy, Authority, Objectivity, Currency and Coverage to make the magnitude of information less confounding. Without having a clear metric standard for measuring the quality, it is hard to recognize the true quality attributes of a website. There is more to a successful website than simply looking attractive or being functional and interactive. Ideally, a successful website is built with a specific strategy in mind, it is focused on usability so that users can navigate the website with success. It incorporates a style that is pleasing to the user's eye and is filled with content that is relevant to the users and is also optimized for search engines. These are a few of the key aspects of a strong website design, complemented by some questions that can be asked when measuring the quality of a website.

Even the most user-friendly and attractive websites are not successful when they are unable to achieve the needs of the organization. The basic questions pertaining to the goal of a library website tend to deal with the following facets:

- What is the nature of the parent organization?
- What is the purpose or goal of the website and does the design of the website succeed in accomplishing this?
- Who is the target audience and how does the design take this into consideration?
- What is the audience expected to do and is this design encouraging them to take that action?

Libraries must set themselves specific website goals to align the design accordingly. The strategy directly influences the design to ensure that the website's purpose is clear and there is no confusion about the content or function. The libraries need to clearly define their target users and constantly check whether the website can accomplish these goals in providing the needs of the target users.

1.2. USABILITY OF A WEBSITE

Usability involves practical considerations like user-friendliness, speed, security, site map and other technical details. If the user is not able to find what they are looking for because of bad navigation, the user will be discouraged and generally leave the site. If a page takes too long to load, not only the user but the search engines will also note the delay and seek alternatives. To evaluate how usable the website is, the following points should be kept in mind.

- Page load speed time
- Ease of navigation
- Availability of search buttons
- Working efficacy of links
- Capacity of library website to work in multiple browsers
- Ability of library website to work on mobile devices

Accessibility falls in the category of usability. The library needs to meet accessibility requirements to ensure that anyone on the internet can easily access it. An individual with any form of mental, physical or cognitive limitations should be able to use the website with little or no alterations. This means that words should be clearly read by the browsers. Creating ALT text on images will allow accessibility software to use the text to audibly describe the images to those who are hearing impaired. Additionally, the website should be accessible with a keyboard, for individuals who lack the ability in their arms or hands.

1.3. CONTENT AND READABILITY OF A WEBSITE

The content made available through the library website should be useful and readable. Content and readability are vital for maximizing the usage of library collections and e-resources. Readability can be ensured by the following:

- Easy to read fonts are used
- Appropriate levels of contrast are maintained between the font colour and the background colour
- Appropriate font size
- Relevant scholarly content
- Content is useful and concise
- Overall design makes the content easy to retrieve.

Apart from aesthetic layout the quality of the content

should be useful enough to pull in the users. Creating content that is consistently relevant will indicate to the users of the website that they can grow to expect the type of rich content that can be found on the website. This would impact positively on the chances that the users will return to the website persistently.

1.4. AESTHETICS OF A WEBSITE

Aesthetic principles guide website design to create a significant impression on the users. The website should be clean, clutter free and complement the content being communicated. Effectiveness of the website's aesthetics can be ensured by:

- Library website's style aligned with the colour, graphics, feel, etc.
- Consistent style throughout entire website
- Website design should be sparse, orderly, formal, clean, tidy and quiet
- Avoid use of unnecessary and excessive images and graphics
- Ensure alignment of the logo and website design

1.5. SEO AND SOCIAL NETWORKING

There are many ways in which the design of a website tends to impact upon the search optimization. SEO and social networking begins with a strong website design which can directly influence the search ranking. The following check list ensures that the website design is optimized:

- Images optimized with ALT tags
- Efficient coding
- Use of relevant keywords in title tags, heading tags, meta-descriptions, etc.
- The library website must have a detailed site map to make the website navigation easy for everyone,

especially those who are using the website with the aid of accessibility software.

When all the facets of the website operate smoothly, the quality of the website increases, thus, bringing in more traffic and eventually leading to increased volume of conversions or completion of intended tasks.

1.6. USING A LIBRARY WEBSITE

The current information overload being experienced by the world needs to be communicated appropriately to the information seekers. Information Communication Technology (ICT) continues to play a vital role in the sharing and exchange of information. The impact of ICT can be seen in every sphere of life today. The World Wide Web has become a popular communication tool for accessing and sharing information on the internet. The easiest way for disseminating and communicating the information is through publication on the websites. The website helps in accessing the vast universe of knowledge prevalent across the globe (Babu, Kumar and Gopal Krishnan, 2009). Library websites have the capacity to bring about a paradigm shift at the higher education levels through rapid technological advancements leading to the evolution from an information society to a knowledge society ("Towards Knowledge Societies," 2002). Libraries are no exception when it comes to the requirement of websites. The development of library websites was initiated way back in the 1990s. As soon as Mosaic, the world's first web browser was released in 1993, academic health science libraries began developing websites (Brower, 2004).

A library website acts as an open forum for the community. A well-equipped library website is the mirror of a library and its services (Konnur, Rajani & Madhusudhan, 2010). From the above discussion, it is clear that library websites have become an absolute necessity. Therefore, it is essential to critically assess the quality of library websites to meet these needs (Dragulanescu, 2002). Webometric tools and techniques are required for assessing website.

1.7. SIGNIFICANCE OF LIBRARY WEBSITE ASSESSMENT

With the advent of library websites most libraries are providing e-data bases, research guides, online technical support, virtual training sessions, online reference chats, citation guides, online courses and subject guides, referencing tools and several more useful services to the users. Thus, the library websites have become the crucial medium of information dissemination.

The current study has facilitated the quality improvement of library websites making them more user-friendly along with having a decisively positive effect on the overall ranking of various institutions. The book will be helpful for the researchers who wish to pursue further research in the area of webometrics. In the current circumstances, it is necessary to assess library websites through webometric techniques like Web Indicators (WIs), Web Analyzers (WAs) and Web Impact Factors (WIFs). The book has identified the challenges, strengths, opportunities and limitations of the library websites. The book will serve as a guideline to librarians and webmasters in the evaluation process from the point of view of design and content management of the libraries in future.

2

Webometrics : A Perspective

2.1. INTRODUCTION

Almind and Ingwersen (1997) coined the term 'Webometrics'. According to them, "The application of informetric methods to World Wide Web (WWW) is called Webometrics". Webometrics is the approach that covers the research of all network based communication using informatics or other quantitative measures.

Bjorneborn and Ingwersen (2001) outlined new directions in webometrics for performing knowledge discovery and tracking issues on the web, based partly on bibliometric methodologies used in bibliographic and citation databases (Bjorneborn & Ingwersen, 2001). They provided a definition of webometrics in their paper entitled, "Towards a basic framework for webometrics" which was published in 2004. According to their definition, "Webometrics is the study of quantitative aspects of the construction and use of information resources, structures and technologies on the web employing bibliometric and informetric approaches. Webometrics involves the study of the web through which one can analyze the number of hyperlinks, type and structure of the hyperlinks, website usage and its effectiveness. Webometrics is evolved from bibliometrics and it covers the concepts of scientometrics and informetrics. Link structure analysis and web technology analysis are the core areas of webometrics". There are several approaches to the comprehensive understanding of webometrics.

2.2. WEBOMETRICS

Webometrics is concisely described as the study of, "Web based content primarily with quantitative methods for social science research using techniques that are not specific to one field of the study" (Bjorneborn & Ingwersen 2001). Webometrics is concerned with measuring various aspects of the web that is; web sites, web pages, words in web pages, hyperlinks and web search engine results. The significance of the web itself as a communication medium for hosting an increasingly wide array of documents ranging from journal articles to brochures has been introduced widely (Thelwall, 2009). Webometrics is a quantitative study of web-related phenomena because of which webometric studies can be applied to the web with commercial search engines for providing raw data. It is almost as widely accepted by researchers as Cybermetrics (Shukla & Tripathi, 2015). Webometrics is the quantitative analysis of web phenomena. It draws upon infometric methods for typically addressing problems related to bibliometrics. Webometrics is triggered off by the realization that the web is an enormous information repository. The web has its own citation indices which are in the form of commercial search engines and are useful for researchers. Among the most visible outputs of webometrics is the ranking of world universities based on their websites and their online impact (Walia & Kaur, 2010).

2.3. WEBOMETRICS ANALYSIS: INSTITUTIONAL AND LIBRARY WEBSITES

For further clarity of comprehension the work has been divided according to webometrics' techniques i.e. Web Indicators, Web Impact Factors and Web Analyzer Test Scores. Categorization has been done according to the level of websites i.e. institutional websites and library websites.

2.3.1. Web Indicators

Jalal, Biswas & Mukhopadhyay (2010) initiated an analysis of the websites of the Central Universities of India. The study collected webometric data through Yahoo and Google search engines using special syntax. An attempt was made to rank the central universities of India using webometric indicators. It was found that the website of the University of Delhi was at the top and the website of Sikkim University was at the bottom in ranking among the central universities of India. The study concluded that more than 75 Indian Universities' websites were underdeveloped and had less than a 100 web pages; therefore, they probably could not qualify for comparative webometric studies. Joicy and Varghese (2011) evaluated the websites of Research and Development Institutions (R&D) in India. The data collection was carried out during the period from 11th March 2011 to 10th April 2011. It was discovered that out of 246 R & D institution websites, 77 or 31.30 percent had proper functional websites. The study revealed that a majority of these institutions provided informative links to contacts, copyright, news and events, Right to Information (RTI) and recorded history. A few websites also provided the opportunity for user interaction in the form of feedback. The study concluded that a majority of these websites were effective and beneficial to the users. Baharum & Jaafar (2013) found that users could form a schema for the location of web objects on institutional websites. The study was investigative and it included a logo, internal links, search, advertisement, external links, login, language and content. There were 94 participants from ten Asian countries who filled the questionnaire followed by a Mock Browser Window consisting of six horizontal and seven vertical grid squares. They completed the survey on the expected location of each of the ten web objects. The study highlighted the fact that the advances of technology significantly affect users' schema for the location of the web object's layout within four years. Gharibeniazi, Kamran & Ghaebi (2015) studied the Iranian State University Websites. According to their study, university websites served as a vital portal for accessing the universities' scientific information for faculty and students. The study compared the evaluation methods like Web Assessment Index (WAI), Web Quality Evaluation Method (WQEM) and Webometrics. The data collection tool (checklist) was prepared by WQEM, WAI and Webometrics. For evaluation of statistical analysis, various parameters like Mean, Standard Deviation and Spearman's Rank Correlation were used. The results of the study based on four main criteria in WQEM indicated that the Iranian State University Websites were well equipped. The Ferdowsi University of Mashhasis stood at first place according to three assessment methods. The hypothesis assumed that there was a positive correlation between WQEM and WAI. The study showed its helpfulness for future university website designers.

Vasantha & Harinarayana (2008) examined 30 global library websites of top science universities. The guidelines given by the National Cancer Institute were applied for assessing the usability features of these websites. Parameters like user experience, link back home, color link navigability and multimedia features were studied. It was found that the time factor had been neglected by all the websites. The navigation feature was observed only in 50 percent of the websites. The study showed that the websites used the facto link color coding and yet the use of multimedia was still to be exploited by these websites. The study concluded that only 30 percent of websites contained both video and audio files. Shukla & Tripathi (2010) examined the status of the content on websites of libraries belonging to Indian academic institutions. The study established a method for measuring Overall Website Performance Calculation (OWPC) and Criteria Wise Website Performance Calculation (CWPC) of the library websites. Further, a comparative study of twenty Central Universities and nineteen Institutes of National Importance including Indian Institutes of Technology (IITs) and Indian Institutes of Management (IIMs) was conducted. It was found that library websites of Institutes of National Importance had better content awareness than central universities according to the identified criteria. The study findings were helpful for librarians and webmasters to improve content awareness status of their library website.

Kalra & Verma (2011) made an attempt to evaluate the library websites of research institutions in India through quantitative and qualitative methods on the basis of Web Impact Factor, a predefined checklist of indicators and an online questionnaire survey. They highlighted the existing procedures and practices of evaluation indicators of websites at the national and international levels. It further revealed that there were many inconsistencies, terminological issues, effective methodologies and techniques for website assessment which were practiced at the international level but were not being used in India. The two major quality components of 'Usability' and 'Usefulness' were studied. The study concluded that there was scope for further research on developing and standardizing indicators with multiple evaluation perspectives at various levels for the benefit of authors. Chow & Commander (2014) examined and highlighted the results of a nationwide study which looked into the design, layout, content, site management and usability of 1469 academic and public library websites from all 50 states in the United States of America. The study designed a Library Website Usability Checklist (LWUC) and conducted an online survey for collecting self reports from academic and public libraries across the United States. Library websites were found to consistently provide information about the hours of operation (97.9 percent), library address (91 percent), news and events (88.9 percent), access to OPAC (84.6 percent), online renewal (77.7 percent), contact information (72.5 percent) and ability to give feedback (74.2 percent). Websites were designed (33 percent) and managed (50 percent) mainly by the librarians as a part of their professional duties and a majority of the websites did not conduct any web usability testing (72.3 percent). The study concluded with certain proposals for library web page design. Wijayaratne & Singh (2015) introduced a library website model. They gave a designer's checklist and an evaluation instrument that were constructed on the basis of the proposed model. The model was developed through a Delphi study that had been attended by two panels of experts from Africa, Europe and America. The authors communicated with the panel via email using two Delphi instruments. The design of these instruments was based on the knowledge gained from surveying the literature and exploring various library websites. A designer checklist of 115 library web content elements and an evaluative instrument were derived from the proposed model during brainstorming sessions. It was concluded that this evaluative instrument could be used in library website evaluation studies for institutional or research purposes while the designer's checklist aimed to assist librarians in designing their library websites. Kaushik (2015) evaluated 28 National Institutes of Technology (NITs) library websites. The study showed that the library website was considered as an effective medium to disseminate diverse forms of information to seekers. Twenty eight NITs library websites were evaluated by using a checklist between February 1 to 28, 2015. The results revealed that the majority of NITs library websites were providing information with regard to their name, logo, about the library book collection, e-resources, accuracy, diverse services and sections. But they lacked in library mission statement, currency, reliability search interfaces, web 2.0 applications and cutting edge technologies like cloud based services. The study concluded that most of the NITs library websites need improvement. In future, this study would also be helpful to judge the quality of a library website. Verma & Devi (2016) discussed Web Content and Design Trends of twelve Indian Institutes of Management (IIMs) Library Websites. A checklist was designed and website optimization.com was used for the data collection. It was found that 12 IIMs library websites were using graphics. The library websites of IIM Calcutta, Lucknow, Udaipur, Shillong and Kashipur provided information only in the English language. A site map was found in all the 12 IIMs library websites. IIM Rohtak, Ranchi, Indore and Udaipur did not provide the feedback link. However, IIMs at Ahmedabad, Calcutta, Lucknow, Udaipur, Shillong did not have the information about the RTI on their websites. IIM Ranchi did not provide information about the maintenance details of the website. The studies emphasized that the IIMs must provide their library websites with attractive and interactivity services which are easily available and accessible for the users. It also stressed the fact that the library web pages should be maintained and updated regularly to enhance demand generation for the library among the users. Mohammed, Garba & Umar (2016) discussed the content of the library websites of 10 universities of Nigeria. A checklist, comprising 43 items was developed, scanned and analyzed at various intervals during December, 2013. The data was presented in tabular form in MS Word. The information provided on these library websites was found to be adequate. Some suggestions were given by the study pertaining to the improvement in the librarian's skills in the area of website development and enhancement of library curriculum in institutions of library instruction to include website development. Gangurde (2017) evaluated the 25 library websites of Management institutes of national and international repute. The study gave the reasons for evaluating the websites and the 25 point scale selected for purposes of ranking and applied to each website of the business schools. Out of 25 library websites, 20 percent were excellent, 56 percent were very good, 8 percent were good and 16 percent belonged to the poor category. The study conclusion showed that the evaluation tools should be used for quality library web pages. Basavaraj (2017) looked at library websites of R & D Institutions of the Government of India. A checklist was designed and a questionnaire was formulated. The questionnaire was administrated to 950 users of which 422 users (44.42 percent) responded from December 2013 to March 2014. The link analysis showed that there were dead links in library websites of:

1. Agriculture (78.72 percent)
2. Natural and Applied Science (77.19 percent)
3. Social Sciences (75 percent)
4. Medical Sciences (58.33 percent)

The study findings showed that library websites of Natural and Applied Sciences were rated to a higher level followed by Medical and Agriculture on the basis of quality of presentation, navigation and other design features. The number of accessibility errors found on the library websites of Agriculture and Medical were high whereas on the library websites of Natural & Applied Sciences and Social Sciences were far lesser. The conclusion highlighted the fact that these library websites should be more user friendly.

2.3.2. Web Impact Factors

Noruzi (2006) investigated Iranian Universities and introduced a new system for measurement of the website i.e. Web Impact Factor (WIF). The study calculated links to the websites of Iranian universities using the Alta Vista search engine. The WIF was calculated by dividing the link page counts by the number of pages found in Alta Vista for every university. The WIF was further compared to study the impact, visibility and influence of Iranian University Websites. The findings showed that these universities had a low in-link WIF due to linguistic reasons because most web pages were in Persian and very few pages were in English. Also the web pages in Persian had a low correlation as compared to English. The reason for this was that the Persian language used by only a small population of the world. Jeyshankar & Babu (2009) explored websites of 45 universities in Tamil Nadu comprising 27 state universities and 18 private universities. Their work identified the domain systems of these websites and analyzed the number of web pages and link pages. The websites were also evaluated through the Web Impact Factor (WIF), Self-link WIF and External Link WIF of the universities' websites in Tamil Nadu. The authors ranked the websites as per the WIF. The study concluded that some universities in Tamil Nadu have a higher number of web pages but their link pages were very less.

Walia & Kaur (2010) resorted to an investigative and observational methodology for examining the government websites in India. The study considered the number of web pages, number of rich files, Web Impact Factor, data analyses and its interpretation. The study highlighted that the performance of these websites was average and required improvements and up gradation. Islam & Tsuji (2011) examined 44 private universities of Bangladesh through webometric indicators and identified the number of web and link pages. The study analyzed and ranked the websites through Alta Vista search engine. It was discovered that some private universities in Bangladesh had a higher number of web pages while their link pages were lesser in number. Thus, the websites fell behind in self-links, external links, Web Impact Factor (WIF) and Overall WIF. The study concluded that these universities did not influence the web and are also not known internationally because of the low self and external links of their websites. Margam & Prakash (2013) explored different characteristics through link analysis of 16 Indian Institutes of Technology (IITs) websites. All the IITs had their own websites working under a Homogeneous Domain Name System (DNS) i.e. .ac.in. The comparisons of ranking of IITs were done using WISER, WIF (In-link) and World Rank. The WISER ranking and WIF (in-link) had Correlation i.e. +0.056 which implied that there was greater association or closeness between two ranking methods. WIF (in-link) rank gave the closer score to the world rank. Hence, IIT Bombay and IIT Madras secured first and second position respectively in WIF (in-link) and in world rank. The study findings guided webmasters to overcome the limitations faced by users and consequently improve their websites. The conclusion was that all websites of IITs could improve their world rank and compete with other top institutions' websites like Harvard University and Massachusetts Institute of Technology. Verma & Brahma (2017) explored the websites of ten Central Universities in North East India. The study calculated the link pages, the number of web pages and analyzed the WIF of these universities. Tezpur University was observed to occupy first place as it had the highest domain and page authority, external equality passing links and total external links. On the other hand Mizoram University topped in internal equality passing links, total equality passing links, total internal links and total links. The WIF of Mizoram University occupied the top position with 83.54 SWIF, 52.731 WIF and 30.80 EWIF as compared to other Central Universities in North East India.

Walia & Gupta (2012) studied the objectives of linking websites of the national libraries through WIF. For analyzing the link structure, data was collected in the months of December 2009, January 2010, April 2010 and May 2010. The study revealed that among select national library websites, the National Libraries of America, Australia and Britain were more visible and hosted more content as compared to the websites of India, Namibia and South Africa. A short survey was conducted to find out the number of functional national library websites in the world. Among 106 National Libraries, 63 National Libraries had Websites. The study highlighted that The Library of Congress had the maximum number of in-links and secured first position whereas National Library of Namibia secured the last rank. Prabakaran & Lihitbar (2015) examined 17 Space Science Library Websites. The data was collected on a number of web pages, external links, in-links, self-links and total links of the websites. Various WIFs were calculated on the basis of the web links and the websites were ranked. The study recommended that there was a need for ranking library websites in space research organizations to serve the users by providing better services. Verma & Brahma (2017) analyzed the number of web pages, link pages and calculated simple WIF, internal link WIF and external link WIF of national libraries in South Asian countries. They ranked the websites as per the WIF. The study used Open Site Explorer Optimization Tool and search engine for the links' analysis. The result visualized that the National Library of India leads with highest domain authority (15.27 percent) and page authority (14.48 percent). The National Library of Sri Lanka had the highest (88.65 percent) internal links. The National Library of India (84.96 percent) had the highest external equity-passing links and total links with 83.69 percent. The National Library of Sri Lanka had the highest (88.65 percent) total internal links and the National Library of India had the highest total external links (84.04 percent) and total links (82.80 percent). The study concluded that the WIF of the National Library of India was the highest followed by the National Library of Sri Lanka and the National Library of Bhutan. Ramanayaka, Chen and Shi (2018) studied the application of Webometric Techniques for measuring and evaluating visibility of University Library Websites in Sri Lanka. The framework for ranking university library websites in Sri Lanka was based on two standard Webometric Methods. The framework was comprised of quantitative web presence specific measuring attributes like: size, visibility, rich files and scholars along with simple and comprehensible mathematical calculations. The library administrators could obtain awareness about whether their website effectively represented itself on the internet with better performance as compared to the ranking results. The findings of the study would guide the librarians to evaluate the strengths and weaknesses according to the performance of their library websites. The effective presence of these library websites on the internet could be taken to be at the top by having proper number of site pages in the websites that impact their perceivability through web search tools and accordingly the quantity of received external links. The study suggested that libraries having low rich files could publish more rich files on the web to improve their overall rank. The research approach criteria and their relative impact provide useful information in monitoring the effectiveness of the current websites and provide strategic suggestions to develop enhanced websites.

2.3.3. Web Analyzers

Islam & Tsuji (2011) evaluated certain university websites in Bangladesh from the perspective of usability. Two online automated tools, namely the HTML Tool Box and Web Analyzer were used along with a questionnaire directed towards the users of these websites. These tools measured the website attributes. The questionnaire was developed and designed based on 23 usability criteria which were grouped into five categories. Each category dealt with one usability aspect. The study showed that the users were not satisfied by the overall usability level of these websites. Only a few of them were satisfied with the available features. There were weaknesses in some aspects of design, interface and performances. The study concluded that it was useful to carry out a more comprehensive study covering more institutions and with increased diagnostic tools to measure the usability of the university websites in Bangladesh. Jeyshankar, Sujitha & Valarmathi (2012) considered the websites of ICMR institutes for their study. They went through the web page size, WAVE Web AIM Accessibility Error; various search engine performances, the difference between pages in various time intervals and a number of rich files. The paper also presented the Link Network Diagram of ICMR Institutes using Pajek Software. The paper concluded that there is a necessity of global level scaling up of all the tools used for website evaluation.

The author has made a pioneering effort in this field pertaining to the assessment and evaluation of library websites using a web analyzer. This has not been attempted ever before.

2.4. EXTRAPOLATION

Sustained observations showed that most of the work is carried on Web Indicators (WIs) followed by Web Impact Factors (WIFs) and Web Analyzers (WAs) or Web Analyzer Test Score (WATS). However, no relevant study was found evaluating library websites through Web Analyzers. Also, none of the work has evaluated library websites using all the three webometrics techniques i.e. WIs, WIFs and WAs/ WATS. This constitutes the research gap. The book has attempted to evaluate the library

3

Webometric Techniques: Web Indicators, Web Impact Factors and Web Analyzer Test Scores

3.1. INTRODUCTION

Webometric tools and techniques provide an in-depth appraisal and analysis of websites. These techniques have the ability to evaluate the performance of a website in terms of capturing user attention, interactive quotient, resolving the scholarly needs, presentations, content coverage, pinpointed search etc. (Jeyashree & Ravichandran, 2013).

websites of Research and Technical Institutions of Ind through all the three Webometric Techniques. Thes techniques include Web Indicators, Web Impact Factor and Web Analyzers which are discussed further in Chapte 3.

3.2. WEB INDICATORS

Web Indicators are a list of synchronous and asynchronous e-resources and services available on a website. These web indicators also highlight the vision and mission of their parent institutions. They cover accuracy, currency, relevance, structure, presentation and maintenance. For the functions, accurate and efficient delivery of library resources and services on the web, the librarians should guide the web developer in designing library web indicators (Kalra & Verma, 2011). These indicators are the checklist (Konnur, Rajani & Madhusudhan, 2010) and web content elements (Wijayaratne & Singh, 2015). They help website managers to understand the relevance and effectiveness of their online initiatives and help them optimize their website. This optimization occurs in the site contents and design. Thus, these indicators provide ample evidence that a certain condition exists for an optimum website and enables webmasters to assess the progress towards the achievement of their objectives. The list of 105 Library Web Indicators has been divided into 5 different blocks. These 5 blocks are Resource, Service, Links, Information and Design as well as Graphics. These have been listed block-wise as follows:

3.2.1. Resource Block

1 E-databases like e-books, e-journals

2 Tutorials on library related topics

3 Dictionaries and encyclopaedias

4 Subject bibliographies and directories

5 Referencing tools

6 Course materials

7 Reading lists recommended by faculty

8 Library glossary

9 Research publications of academic staff

10 Past years question papers and assignments

11 Newspaper clippings

12 New arrivals

13 Online reference chat

14 Library podcast

3.2.2. Service Block

15 OPAC (Online Public Access Catalogue)

16 Inter library loans service

17 Online feedbacks

18 Online book reservation

19 E-mail reference of librarian

20 Users training sessions

21 Online orientation session

22 Document delivery service

23 Communication forums

3.2.3. Links Block

24 Links to the course and study program sites

25 Link to parent institution's homepage

26 Links to information manuals like library brochure, etc.

27 Free internet resources of general interest

28 Links to download necessary software tools

29 Links to popular internet search engines and web directories

30 Links to related sites of local and international libraries

31 Links to OPACs of other libraries

3.2.4. Information Block

32 Vision and Mission Statement

33 Floor plan

34 Campus site map

35 Web masters contact details

36 Short biographies of staff members

37 Photographs of staff members

38 Frequently used visitors' number

39 Help guides and instructions for online and in-house services

40 Contact information

41 Library opening hours

42 Library staff directory

43 Copyright statement

44 Library holiday-calendar

45 Policies, rules and regulations

46 Online and in-house facilities

47 Library news, special events, library bulletin and notices

48 Library history

49 FAQs

50 Institutions full name

51 Library policies

3.2.5. Design & Graphic Block

52 Memorable URL

53 Website should be consistent in layout

54 Hyperlinks identity (to describe the targeted web page)

55 Home page length is within one screen

56 Date of last website update is provided

57 Avoid use of flash animation

58 Avoid use of background sounds

59 Avoid horizontal scrolling

60 Access home page from all other pages

61 Accessible through Chrome and Firefox
62 Provides text only options for pages
63 Use descriptive headings, titles and tabs
64 Use heading tag consistently
65 Functional through the use of a keyboard
66 Provide multilingual access options
67 Do not blink, flash or move the text or images
68 Write abbreviations and acronyms fully in the first instance
69 Do not use underline unless it is a hyperlink
70 Use high contrast between text and backgrounds
71 Avoid long text blocks
72 Headlines to support Meta tag
73 Use left justify text and headlines
74 Strong visual identity
75 Use visual consistency across all pages
76 Include links to return to library home page
77 Well designed screen
78 Consistent navigation
79 Internal search engine
80 Short menus consisting of 5-7 links
81 Multiple access for services and facilities
82 Use navigational aids e.g. "bread crumbs" like return to top, next, previous
83 Relative font size
84 Headings for Table
85 Large graphics (more than 200kb)
86 Avoid non standard HTML codes
87 Headlines that support scanning
88 Do not present information through color
89 Avoid use of titles like "click here" and "see more"

90 Use large clickable areas or hotspots
91 Print friendly function
92 Avoid italics for large text blocks
93 Line length within 10-12 words per line
94 Font type "Georgia" or "Verdana" for web pages
95 Use graphics
96 Font type "Times New Roman" for heavy text
97 Include anchor links for important links
98 Client site image map
99 Homepage within 800*600 pixels
100 Content of pages does not require scrolling
101 Sufficient space for links
102 Leave space between letters of acronym
103 Limit page to 200kb of graphics
104 TARGET-main arguments to link tags
105 Navigation bars at the bottom of the page

3.3. WEB IMPACT FACTORS

The feasibility and reliability of calculating impact factor for the website is called Web Impact Factor (WIF). It contains quantitative indicators developed by Ingwersen (1998). According to him, WIF is calculable and reliable if processed by means of a series of inverted but identical Boolean Operations, with caution, in order to isolate and estimate the number of web pages pointing to the pages at a given site.

WIF is the snapshot of a search engine database in a specific time. The WIF is based on an analogy between hyperlinks and citations and is the adaptation of the 'Impact Factor' for the web. Thus, WIF is the number of outside web pages linking to a website which is divided by the number of web pages in that very website at a given time. It provides quantitative tools for ranking, evaluating, categorizing and comparing websites. The WIF analysis presents a methodology for evaluating international visibility, impact of institutional websites and their connections with other websites. It measures the use and popularity of institutions on the web and can be regarded as a tool for measuring the accuracy of search engine performance, website organization besides linking and structuring of pages. Based on the links of the websites, there are two more types of WIFs i.e. Revised Web Impact Factor (R-WIF) and Overall Web Impact Factor (O-WIF) (Noruzi, 2006).

WIF has served as an indexing tool where the ratio of links and web pages is initiated. There are three types of WIFs based on the different types of links. These links are as follows :

Back or In-Links : The Back or In-Links are incoming hyperlinks of existing website to another website.

Self-Links : Self-Links are links to the web page itself. They are links that link one page to another page on the same website.

The three types of WIFs are as follows :

3.3.1. WIF

Total link pages (in-links and self-links pages) divided by web pages

3.3.2. Revised WIF (R-WIF)

In-link pages divided by web pages

3.3.3. Overall WIF (O-WIF)

Self-link pages divided by web pages

Google Search Engine is used to collect data .i.e. number of web pages, the number of self-links and the number of in-links.

WP (Web Pages) = Total number of web pages extracted from Google for example domain (pkklib.iitk.ac.in)

SL (Self-Link) = Number of self-links extracted from Google for example link domain: (pkklib.iitk.ac.in AND domain: pkklib.iitk.ac.in)

IL (In-Link) = Number of in-links extracted from Google for example link domain: (pkklib.iitk.ac.in NOTdomain: pkklib.iitk.ac.in)

3.4. WEB ANALYZER TEST SCORES

Web Analyzers are another source for evaluating websites. They evaluate those indicators which cannot be evaluated by human eyes. Thus, they help to get insights on the performance of the website. Like web indicators, web analyzers also assist in optimizing site performance by eliminating navigational bottlenecks, identifying best sources of acquisition and helping to gauge traffic. They also provide a list of errors that are detected on web pages as also get valuable reports and statistics about the websites. There are a number of online software programs to evaluate websites. They keep a track of the websites and their problems. They also investigate back links, broken links, external and internal links, page speed, load time, mobile compatibility, domain age, keyword consistency, Search Engines Optimization (SEO) Tools, hit counts, etc. ("Web Analytics Definitions - Digital Analytics Association," 2007). Some of the web analyzers are GT Matrix, Ahrefs, Sitebeam, etc. Sitebeam 5.2.1 was used to test the library websites of Research and Technical Institutions of India. This version was released on 26th March 2014. A maximum of 100 web pages of a website were tested by Sitebeam. Each library website was tested on 26 individual test scores ranging from 0 to 10. These tests are as follows :

Alternative Text Test : Alternative Text depicts the type of images contained in the website.

Amount of Content Test : It measures the volume of text content on a website. The score is derived entirely from the total word count.

Analytics Test : Analytics allow for detailed analysis of user behavior.

Broken Links Test : Broken links are links to web addresses that do not exist or show an error.

Domain Age Test : Domain age is a key factor that depicts the trust of a website.

Error Pages Test : Check for error messages and faults of a website.

Facebook Test : Check whether the website has a Facebook page.

Freshness Test : It determines how frequently and substantially a website appears to be keeping up to date and fresh.

Headings Test : Tests whether or not properly defined headings are used by the website and lists them. Good use of headings has a positive effect on search engine rankings.

Incoming Links Test : It counts the number of links found pointing to a website and compares them against other sites. Websites with many links generally score much higher.

Missing Files Test : Detection of missing files within a website.

Mobile Test : Tests whether a website is optimized for mobile and tablet devices.

Open Graph Test : It checks how the website appears when shared on social networking sites.

Popularity Test : It tests how popular a website is as compared to other websites.

Printability Test : It tests whether or not pages are designed for printing and shows how the homepage appears when printed.

Readability Test : Measures how easily the information written on a website is comprehended.

Redirection Test : It tests whether the website uses client side redirection and prevents users from using the back button.

Search Engine Results Test : Displays how the website will typically appear in the results of a search engine like Google.

Social Interest Test : It measures the amount of social interest that individual pages have within the website.

Speed Test : Measures the speed of the website, including factors like file size and application response time.

Spelling Test : This test checks for spelling errors. Poor spelling leaves a poor impression of the website. Poor spellings can also make the content difficult to understand.

Stylesheets Test : Tests whether the web pages are built properly using Cascading Style Sheets (CSS). CSS are a standard means for building web pages.

Twitter Test : Checks whether a website has a Twitter account and how that account compares with that of other websites.

Typosquatting Test : Tests whether likely variations (typos) of the domain name for this website are registered. This practice is known as typosquatting.

URL Chopping Test : Tests whether URLs (web addresses) work when pieces are chopped off. It is surprisingly common for users to condense for example: www.example.com/news/article1 invariably becomes: www.example. com/ news/.

W3C Compliance Test : Tests whether the website is W3C compliant. W3C is the primary standard set for the web and defines the precise specification of how the HTML (or XHTML) of a website should be written to ensure compatibility, accessibility and following of best practices.

4

Library Websites: Qualitative and Quantitative Assessment

4.1. INTRODUCTION

Five Webometric Techniques were used for conducting a Qualitative and Quantitative Assessment of Library Websites of Research and Technical Institutions of India. These five techniques for data collection were:

(i) Web Indicators (WIs)

(ii) Web Impact Factor (WIF)

(iii) Revised Web Impact Factor (RWIF)

(iv) Overall Web Impact Factor (OWIF)

(v) Web Analyzer Test Scores (WATS)

To successfully examine the library websites through Web Indicators the author prepared a single nonoverlapping list of 105 Web Indicators based on two significant studies of Wijayayaratne and Wilson (2015). The Web Analyzer (WA) Sitebeam was also used for the study as its 26 tests were applied on the library websites. The data collected and evaluated was on the basis of the library websites of Research and Technical Institutions of India with WIFs. In addition, the Composite Rank was calculated by summing up the scores of all the above mentioned five evaluative techniques.

A vast range of 105 Web Indicators was taken up which was categorized into five different blocks namely:

(i) Resource (14 Indicators)

(ii) Service (9 Indicators)

(iii) Links (8 Indicators)

(iv) Information (20 Indicators)

(v) Design & Graphics (54 Indicators)

For ease of understanding, each library website was at first sorted on the basis of the available and missing indicators from among the list of 105 Web Indicators. Observations showed that the Web Indicators were examined on library websites during the period ranging from 4th February 2017 to 24th March 2017.

The library websites considered under the study were evaluated through Web Analyzer Test Scores (WATS). A maximum of 100 web pages were tested by the Sitebeam Web Analyzer. Each library website was tested on 26 individual tests scores ranging from 0 to 10. These scores were further divided into 3 parts like high score (scoring from 10 to 7), average score (scoring from 6.9 to 4) and low score (scoring from 3.9 to 0). Thus, the library website can score a maximum of 260. The Web Analyzer Tests were applied on the library websites on 24th January 2017 and 3rd February 2017 respectively.

Web Impact Factor, Revised Web Impact Factor and Overall Web Impact Factor of each library website was calculated with the help of web search engine i.e. Google using the Boolean Operators "OR", "NOT", "AND". All three Web Impact Factors have been calculated from 25th March 2017 to 5th April 2017.

4.2. LIST OF LIBRARY WEBSITES

There are different forms of rankings published by various international bodies including the Academic Ranking of World Universities (ARWU), Shanghai as well as Times Higher Education Ranking (THE) and the National Institutional Ranking Framework (NIRF). These ranking methodologies are based on indicators like teaching, learning resources, research and professional practices, outreach and perception but these have not considered the website as a solo indicator for ranking. The Ranking Web of Universities (RWU), however, has evaluated websites of universities of the world since 2004 for the Cyber Metric Lab Spanish National Research Council (CSIC). It is one of the largest academic website rankings of Higher Educational Institutions (HEIs) of the world. It provides ranking twice a year i.e. in January and July. This study has considered library websites of the top 25 Research and Technical Institutions of India according to the Ranking Web of Universities (RWU) in January 2017. The list of library websites of these institutions as per their Institutional Rank (IR) is given in Table 4.1 below:

Table 4.1. Ranking of 25 Research and Technical Institutions of India

IR	*Library Website*	*URL*	*Abbreviation*
1.	IIT Bombay	library.iitb.ac.in	IITBLW
2.	IIT Kanpur	pkklib.iitk.ac.in	IITKLW
3.	IIT Madras	cenlib.iitm.ac.in	IITMLW
4.	IIT Delhi	library.iitd.ac.in	IITDLW
5.	Tata Institute of Fundamental Research, Mumbai	tifr.res.in	TIFRMLW

6.	IIT Kharagpur	library.iitkgp.ernet.in	IITKGLW
7.	IIT Roorkee	mgcl.iitr.ac.in	IITRLW
8.	IIT Guwahati	iitg.ac.in	IITGLW
9.	NIT Rourkela	library.nitrkl.ac.in	NITRLW
10.	Jawaharlal Nehru Centre for Advanced Scientific Research	jncasr.ac.in	JNCASRLW
11.	NIT Trichy	nitt.edu	NITTLW
12.	BITS Pillani	bits-pilani.ac.in	BITPLW
13.	International Institute of Information Technology, Hyderabad	oldwww.iiit.ac.in	IIITHLW
14.	NIT Calicut	library.nitc.ac.in	NITCLW
15.	The Institute of Mathematical Sciences	imsc.res.in	IMSCLW
16.	Indian Agricultural Research Institute	iari.res.in	IARILW
17.	IIT Hyderabad	library.iith.ac.in	IITHLW
18.	ISB Hyderabad	isb.edu	ISBHLW
19.	IIM Ahmedabad	iima.ac.in	IIMALW
20.	Indian Institutes of Science Education and Research Kolkata	iiserkol.ac.in	IISERKLW
21.	IISER Pune	iiserpune.ac.in	IISERPLW
22.	NIT Karnataka	library.nitk.ac.in	NITKLW
23.	IIT Bhuvnashwar	library.iitbbs.ac.in	IITBBSLW
24.	Thapar University	thapar.edu	THULW
25.	Saha Institute of Nuclear Physics	wbpublibnet.gov.in	SINPLW

4.3. LIBRARY WEBSITES : ASSESSMENT

The Library Websites were evaluated through Web Indicators, Web Analyzer Test Scores and Web Impact

Factors. A Composite Rank (CR) was determined after consolidating the individual scores obtained through three techniques i.e. Web Indicators, Web Analyzer Test Scores (WATS) and Web Impact Factors. The Assessment process has been delineated institution wise.

4.3.1. IIT Bombay Library Website (IITBLW)

Out of 105 Web Indicators, 68 (65 percent) were found to be available and 37 (35 percent) were missing from the IITBLW. The Service Block scored the highest i.e. 77.77 percent. It contained inter library loan, online book reservation, online orientation programs and sessions, etc. However, the online feedback, digital communication forum were not available on IITBLW. The Link Block had the second highest score i.e. 75 percent. It contained links to course and study as well as programs sites as also the links to related sites while IITBLW is deficient in links to the information manuals like the library brochure, etc. Next is the Information Block with a score of 70 percent. It contains short staff bibliographies, institution's full name, library history, etc. The short-comings of IITBLW are the absence of the vision and mission statement of the library, library policies and FAQs. The Design and Graphics Block scored 68.5 percent. It is equipped with memorable URL, consistent IITBLW layout, etc. and yet IITBLW lacked in homepage length, date of last IITBLW update, etc. The Resource Block performed poorly. It scored 28.57 percent and included e-data bases, the tutorials on library related topics, dictionaries and encyclopaedias, etc. The web indicators like library glossary, research publications of academic staff were not mentioned explicitly on IITBLW. Out of a total 26 tests, IITBLW scored high in 14 tests like alternative text; the amount of content, analytics, etc. It has scored average in two tests namely broken links and incoming links. It has scored low in 10 tests namely, Facebook, missing files, printability, etc. The score on 260 is 153.9 (59.19

percent). Also 100 pages were tested on 24th January 2017. The IITBLW has been deserved to be using Word Press Content Management System because of which the writing of IITBLW is quite easy to understand. While 88 percent of IITBLW is using Google Analytics, 96.4 percent of IITBLW is using alternative text. It is updated after every 2 to 3 days. There are 146 other websites which are linked to IITBLW. Thus, 90 percent pages of IITBLW have proper headings and it has been ranked 7309th on the Alexa. While 9 percent of IITBLW is using tables for layout. There were 89 missing files observed over 87 pages. It has 51 internal and 01 external broken links out of the 1709 links tested by Sitebeam. All these missing files, broken links tend to slow down IITBLW. It shares 05 pages on Facebook. IITBLW has a Twitter account with 213 Tweets. It showed very less W3C Compliance, which means that it has less accessibility and is not compatible with more browsers. Very few pages of IITBLW have appeared in the search engine results. It has not used the Open Graph tag and is not optimized for printing. IITBLW had 1535 spelling errors and takes 6.8 seconds to download and 0.8 seconds to upload the pages of IITBLW. IITBLW has a WIF score of 0.0003, RWIF score of 0.0001 and OWIF score of 0.0002 respectively.

The Composite Rank (CR) is calculated by adding WI, WATS, WIF, RWIF and OWIF and then dividing them with five to get the mean score where WI score is 68 out of 105, WATS is 153.9 out of 260 and WIF score is 0.0003, RWIF score is 0.0001 and OWIF score is 0.0002. So, the total score of all the five evaluative techniques is 221.9 and the mean score is 44.4. The Composite Rank is 4 and Institutional Rank is 1.

4.3.2. IIT Kanpur Library Website (IITKLW)

Out of 105 web indicators, 69 (66 percent) are present and 36 (34 percent) are missing from IITKLW. The Links Block has the highest scores i.e. 87.5 percent.

Links connected with the IITKLW are linked to study programs, parent institutions, etc. However link to information manual like the library brochure is unavailable. The Information Block scored second highest with 75 percent. It included the Mission Statement of the library, the availability of short biographies and photographs of the staff members, etc. However the webmaster's contact details, campus site map, etc. are missing. The Design and Graphics Block scored third position with a score of 64.81 percent. It included memorable URL; IITKLW is consistent in layout, etc. On the other hand, date of the last IITKLW update, details of avoiding usage of flash animation are not available on IITKLW. The fourth position is securéd by the Service Block a score of 55.55 percent. It includes OPAC, online feedback, etc. However, inter-library loan, virtual users training session, online orientation session, etc. are also not available on IITKLW. The last position is secured by the Resource Block having a 50 percent score. It includes e-databases, subject bibliographies, referencing tools; course material etc. but library podcast, online reference chat, newspaper clippings, etc. were unavailable on IITKLW. Out of the total 26 tests, IITKLW scored the highest in 15 tests like the amount of content, alternative text, mobile, etc. Its score has been average in 3 tests like open graphs, speed, broken links, etc. and the score is low in 8 tests including W3C Compliance, analytics, Twitter, etc. The score from 260 is 161.6 (62.15 percent). The 100 pages of IITKLW were tested on 24th, January 2017. IITKLW has 28 Internal and 51 external broken links out of the total 4122 links tested by Sitebeam. IITKLW has not used Open Graph tags and 96 percent of the website is written using Cascading Style Sheet for its construction in HTML. IITKLW has used the Joomla Content Management System. Only 3 percent of the images have not used specified alternative text. On an average, its pages take 4.9 seconds to download and 0.5

seconds per page to upload. Most headings are defined properly and 95 percent of the IITKLW is optimized for printing. The IITKLW pages used 97 percent of external style sheets and the domain age is 12.9 years. It has been optimized for mobile and tablet devices. Only 05 links of other websites are present in IITKLW which does not use any analytical software. From top 8 pages of IITKLW, 12 files are missing. No page is W3C Compliant. While it does not have any Twitter account two pages are shared on Facebook. IITKLW has 7211 potential spelling errors. The IITKLW is updated after every 4.2 months and 18.4 percent of the headings are empty or incorrectly defined. It is ranked 7781st in world popularity by Alexa. Only 1 percent of IITKLW used Tables for layout. The IITKLW has a WIF score of 0.13, RWIF score of 0.07 and an OWIF score of 0.06 respectively.

The Composite Rank (CR) is calculated by adding WI, WATS, WIF, RWIF and OWIF and then dividing them with five to get the mean score where WI score is 69 out of 105, WATS is 161.6 out of 260, WIF score is 0.13, RWIF score is 0.07 and OWIF score is 0.06. Thus, the total score from all five evaluative techniques is 230.9 and the mean score is 46.2. Both the Composite and Institutional Ranks are same i.e. 2.

4.3.3. IIT Madras Library Website (IITMLW)

Out of 105 web indicators, 57 (54 percent) are available and 48 (46 percent) are not available or are missing from IITMLW. Links Block has scored the highest score with 62.5 percent. It includes the link to the parent institution's homepage, the links to OPAC of other libraries, etc. However, the links to popular internet search engines, links to information manuals, etc. are missing from IITMLW. The second highest score is of the Design & Graphics Block having 61.11 percent scores. It includes memorable URL, date of last IITMLW update, avoidance of use of flash animation, etc. whereas multilingual access options, etc. are missing from IITMLW. Next block is Service Block with a score of 55.55 percent. It includes availability of OPAC; inter library loan, document delivery service, etc. while online book reservation, virtual users training session, etc. are missing from the IITMLW. The fourth position is secured by the Information Block having a 55 percent score. It includes the floor plan of the library, short biographies of staff members, institution's full name, etc. However, campus sitemap, web masters contact details; visitor's number count, etc. are not available in IITMLW. The last position held among the 5 blocks is Resource Block with 21.42 percent. It includes e-databases, e-books, e-journals, referencing tools, course materials, etc. However, the tutorials on library related topics, reading list recommended by the faculties, subject bibliographies and directories, library podcast, etc. are missing from the IITMLW. Out of 26 tests, IITMLW has scored the highest in 10 tests that include domain age, error pages, the amount of content, etc. It has scored average in 2 tests like URL format and readability. It has scored low in 14 tests and these are broken links, analytics, alternative text, etc. The score on 260 is 125.1 (48.11 percent). Around 94 pages of IITMLW were tested on 24th January 2017. The IITMLW was observed to have 24 internal and 92 external broken links out of 1613 links tested by Sitebeam. There were 80.9 percent pages which used Cascading Style Sheet for layout of IITMLW. On an average its pages take 1.5 seconds to download and 0.4 seconds to upload. IITMLW is ranked 6736th in the world for popularity according to Alexa. Some of the pages of IITMLW are traced in the search engine results. On an average, the IITMLW is updated every 2 weeks, the domain age is 13.9 years and the expiry date is 28/02/19. Another 88 websites are linked to the IITMLW. No analysis software is used by IITMLW. It does not have any Twitter account but 13 pages have been shared on Facebook. No Open Graph tag was used. Alternative Text is used rarely i.e.

96.1 percent of the images do not have alternative text, while 86.2 percent of the pages are not using proper headings. The IITMLW has 405 spelling errors and it is not optimized for mobile and tablet devices. About 19.1 percent of the IITMLW is using Tables for layout. This website is neither W3C Compliant nor optimized for printing. The IITMLW has a WIF score of 1.04, the RWIF score is 0.42 and OWIF score is 1.04 respectively.

The Composite Rank (CR) is calculated by adding WI, WATS, WIF, RWIF and OWIF and then dividing them with five to get the mean score where WI score is 57 out of 105, WATS is 125.1 out of 260, while the WIF score is 1.04 while RWIF score is 0.42 and the OWIF score is 1.04. So, the total score of all the five evaluative techniques is 184.6 and the average is 36.9. The Composite Rank is 22 and the Institutional Rank is 3.

4.3.4. IIT Delhi Library Website (IITDLW)

Among 105 web indicators, 64 (61 percent) were available and 41 (39 percent) are missing in the IITDLW. Link and Information Block scored the highest at 75 percent. The Links Block included links to free internet resources, etc. whereas the links to popular internet search engines, web directories, etc. are missing from the IITDLW. The Information Block included the floor plan of the library, visitor's number count, staffwith photographs, etc. while campus sitemap, Vision and Mission Statement of the library, web masters contact details, FAQs, etc. are missing from the IITDLW. The second highest score is of Design & Graphics Block with 61.11 percent score that includes memorable URL, date of last IITDLW update, avoiding usage of background sound, etc. But hyperlinks identity, large graphics, etc. are not involved in IITDLW. The fourth position is of Service Block which scored 44.44 percent. It includes OPAC, inter library loan, online book reservation, etc. while digital communication forum, virtual users' training session, online feedback etc. were missing. The last position among the 5 blocks is that of the Resource Block with a score of 42.85 percent. It included e-data bases, e-books, e-journals, referencing tools, etc, and lacked in tutorials on library related topics, new arrival lists, library podcast etc. Out of 26 tests, IITDLW scored the highest in 13 tests like domain age, error pages, the amount of content, etc. It scored average level in 4 tests like incoming links, social interest, style sheet, etc. It had a low score in 11 tests which were alternative text, analytics, broken links, etc. The score on 260 is 128.8 (49.53 percent). There were 57 pages of IITDLW that were tested on 24th January 2017. The IITDLW has 4 Internal and 69 external broken links out of a total of 683 links tested by Sitebeam. Another fact is that 46 percent of the IITDLW is written using HTML and 39 percent is written using XHTML1 and 15 percent is written using unspecified HTML. Also 54.4 percent of IITDLW used Tables for layout wherein 98.2 percent of IITDLW pages used external stylesheets. On an average pages take 1.7 seconds to download and 0.4 seconds per page to upload. The website is updated every 1.1 months. The domain age is 13.9 years of IITDLW and its expiry date is 28/02/19. It is optimized for mobile and tablet devices via 'responsive' design. It has been ranked 9205th in the world for popularity by Alexa. There are 82 other websites linked to the IITDLW. It has no Twitter account but shares 3 pages on Facebook. No defined headings are used in 89.5 percent of the pages. IITDLW is neither optimized for printing nor is W3C Compliant. Its 97.9 percent images do not have alternative text. Only 2.1 percent of IITDLW has valid alternative text. 1.8 percent of the IITDLW is using Google Analytical whereas some pages of IITDLW can be traced in search engine results. IITDLW does not use any Open Graph Tags or Content Management System. There are 6 missing files spread over 05 pages. The IITDLW has a WIF score of 2.08, an RWIF score of 1.32 and an OWIF score as of 0.76

respectively.

The Composite Rank is calculated by adding the WI, WATS, WIF, RWIF and OWIF and then dividing them with five to get the mean score where the WI score is 64 out of 105, WATS is 128.8 out of 260, WIF is 2.08, RWIF is 1.32 and OWIF is 0.76. The total score of all five evaluative techniques is 197.0 and the mean score is 39.4. The Composite Rank is 12 and the Institutional Rank is 4.

4.3.5. Tata Institute of Fundamental Research, Mumbai Library Website (TIFRMLW)

Out of 105 web indicators, 37 (35 percent) are available and 68 (65 percent) are missing from the TIFRMLW. The Design & Graphics Block has scored the highest with 53.70 percent. It includes memorable URL; hyperlinks identity, provides text only options for pages, etc. while date of the last TIFRMLW update, providing multilingual access options, etc. are not included in the TIFRMLW. The second highest score is obtained by the Service Block with 33.33 percent score. It includes online feedback, email reference of the librarian, virtual users training session, etc. But OPAC, inter library loan, online book reservation, etc. are not included on the TIFRMLW. The third position is attained by the Resource Block with a score of 14.2 percent. It contains e-databases, e-books, e-journals, referencing tools while the tutorials on library related topics, subject bibliographies, etc. are missing from the TIFRMLW. Next block is the Links Block with a score of 12.5 percent. It includes a link to the parent institution's homepage. However, links to OPAC of other libraries, links to course and study program sites, etc. are missing from the TIFRMLW. The last position among the 5 blocks is Information Block with a 10 percent score. It includes the institution's name, online and in house facilities, etc. But mission statement and the floor plan of the library, campus sitemap, etc. are missing. Out of 26 tests, TIFRMLW has scored the highest in 12 tests namely the amount of content, domain age, error pages, etc. It has an average score in 5 tests like incoming links, popularity, etc. It has scored low in 9 tests and these are analytics, broken links, Facebook, etc. The score from 260 is 135.6 (52.15 percent). There were 100 pages of TIFRMLW which were tested on 24th January 2017. While 48 percent of the TIFRMLW is written using HTML4 and 44 percent is written in HTML5 while 8 percent is written in unspecified HTML. The TIFRMLW makes use of Open Graph tags. Only 41 percent of TIFRMLW is optimized for printing. There are 999 other websites linked to the TIFRMLW. On an average, pages take 2.8 seconds to download and 10.2 seconds to upload. The TIFRMLW is updated every 5 days. The domain age is 12.1 years and expiry date is 30/04/24. It has been optimized for mobile and tablet devices via 'responsive' design. It has 78 internal and 100 external broken links out of a total of 2534 links tested by Sitebeam. TIFRMLW has no Twitter account but 12 percent of TIFRMLW is shared on Facebook. There are 112 missing files spread over 33 pages. Only 2 percent of TIFRMLW uses some form of analytical software. There are 1118 spelling errors on TIFRMLW. There are 97 percent of the pages which are not W3C Compliant. Also 55 percent of the pages do not have proper headings. Very few pages of the TIFRMLW can be traced in search engine results. There are 43.2 percent of images that do not have alternative text. There is also 26 percent of the TIFRMLW which is using Tables for layout but does not use any Content Management System. TIFRMLW has a WIF score of 3.01, RWIF score of 1.93 and OWIF score of 1.08 respectively.

The Composite Rank is calculated by adding WI, WATS, WIF, RWIF and OWIF and then dividing them with five to get the mean score where the WI score is 37 out of 105, WATS is 135.6 out of 260, WIF score is 3.01, RWIF score is 1.93 and OWIF score is 1.08. Thus, the total score of all the five evaluative techniques is 178.6 and the mean score is 35.7. The Composite Rank is 24 and the Institutional Rank is 5.

4.3.6. IIT Kharagpur Library Website (IITKGLW)

Out of 105 web indicators, 58 (55 percent) are available and 47 (45 percent) are missing from IITKGLW. The Service Block has scored the highest with 66.66 percent. It contains OPAC, online feedback, inter-library loan, e-mail reference of the librarian, etc. However, online book reservation, digital communication forums, online orientation sessions, etc. were missing from the IITKGLW. The second highest score was obtained by the Links Block securing 62.5 percent. It contains the link to parent institution's homepage, the links to study program sites, etc. But the links to related sites, the links to information manuals, etc. were all missing from the IITKGLW. Next is the Information Block with 60 percent score. It includes library history, short biographies and photographs of the staff members, etc. though the floor plan, campus sitemap; visitor's number count, etc. are not available on it. It is followed by the Design & Graphics Block having a score of 53.7 percent. It includes memorable URL, avoidance of horizontal scrolling, etc. where as the homepage length is within one screenful of information and date of last IITKGLW update, etc. are missing. The last position among the 5 blocks is of the Resource Block with a score of 42.85 percent. It includes e-databases, subject bibliographies and directories, referencing tools, course materials, etc. though the tutorials on library related topics, lists recommended by the faculties, library podcast, etc. are missing. Out of 26 tests, the IITKGLW has scored the highest in 11 tests like domain age, error pages, freshness, etc. It has scored average in 7 tests like the amount of content, URL format, headings, etc. It has scored low in 8 tests and these are Facebook, broken links, analytics, etc. The score on 260 is 150 (57.69 percent). In all 16 pages of IITKGLW have been tested on 24th January 2017. It does not use any recognized analytics software. The IITKGLW has 4 internal and 5 external broken links out of 94 links tested by Sitebeam. It had no Twitter account but shared three pages on the Facebook. IITKGLW had 92 spelling errors. None of the pages is W3C Compliant. While 81 percent of the IITKGLW is written using XHTML1 and 19 percent is written using unspecified HTML. Only 6.3 percent of the IITKGLW is optimized for printing. Also 88.9 percent of the images do not have alternative text. Very few pages in the IITKGLW have been traced in the search engine results. However, the IITKGLW is not using any Open Graph tags, although some basic information is inferred from other tags. The IITKGLW is not optimized for mobile and tablet devices. There are 106 websites links to IITKGLW. There are 12.5 percent of the pages which are not using any defined headings. On an average the pages take 1.8 seconds to download and 0.4 seconds per page to upload. On an average IITKGLW is updated after every 1.7 weeks. The domain age is 11.9 years. The IITKGLW uses the Drupal Content Management System. The IITKGLW has WIF score of 0.0004, RWIF score of 0.0002 and an OWIF score of 0.0002 respectively.

The Composite Rank is calculated by adding WI, WATS, WIF, RWIF and OWIF and then dividing them with five to get the mean score where WI score is 58 out of 105, WATS is 150 out of 260, WIF score is 0.0004, RWIF score is 0.0002 and OWIF score is 0.0002. Thus, the total score of all the five evaluative techniques is 208.0 and the average is 41.6. The Composite Rank is 8 and the Institutional Rank is 6.

4.3.7. IIT Roorkee Library Website (IITRLW)

Out of 105 web indicators, 78 (74 percent) are available and 27 (26 percent) are missing from the IITRLW with block wise results as follows: Research 9 (64.28 percent), Service 6 (66.66 percent), Link 7 (87.5 percent), Information 13 (65 percent) and Design & Graphics 43 (79.6 percent) respectively. The Links Block attained the highest score i.e. 87.5 percent. It includes the link to parent institutions, free internet usage, etc. However, the links to information manuals is unavailable on the IITRLW. Design & Graphics Block scored the second highest i.e. 79.6 percent. It includes availability of memorable URL. The IITRLW is consistent in layout, etc. but the home page length is within one screenful of information while the date of the last IITRLW update is not present on the site. The Service Block scored 66 percent and attained third position. It includes OPAC, online feedback, online book reservations, etc. But the inter-library loan, email references of the librarian are missing from the IITRLW. The Information Block has scored 65 percent and attained the fourth position. It included the floor plan of the library, short bibliographies, etc. What was missing, however, was the vision campus sitemaps, webmasters contact details, library staff directories, etc. The Resource Block attained the last position and scored 64.28 percent. It contained e-databases, subject bibliography, reference tools, a list of new arrivals, etc. However, the IITRLW did not have library tutorials, dictionaries and library glossary. Out of 26 tests, the IITRLW scored the highest in 9 tests which include domain age, error pages, freshness, etc. It scored an average in 4 tests like the amount of content, headings, etc, and scored low in 13 tests which included analytics, Facebook, broken links, etc. The score in 260 was 119.4 (45.92 percent). There were 26 pages of the IITRLW which were tested on 24th January 2017. The IITRLW has only 7 internal and 23 external links broken from among 199 links tested by Sitebeam. On an average, the pages took 2.8 seconds to download and 0.4 seconds per page to upload. There was 65.4 percent of the IITRLW that used Cascading Style Sheet. There were 73.1 percent of the pages which used external stylesheets. The IITRLW is ranked 11894th in the world of popularity according to Alexa. The IITRLW is updated every 1.4 months. It is not using any recognized analytics software. While it has no Twitter account, there are two pages of the IITRLW which have been shared on the Facebook. The IITRLW had 22 missing files which are spread over 18 pages. There were 265 potential spelling errors. Very few pages of the IITRLW were traced in the search engine results. A majority of the pages, i.e. 88.5 percent, are not W3C Compliant while 62 percent of the IITRLW is written using XHTML1 and 30 percent is written using HTML5 whereas 8 percent had used HTML4. Only 30.8 percent of the IITRLW is optimized for printing. A majority of the images do not have alternative text. The IITRLW does not use Open Graph tags, although some basic information could be inferred from other tags. There are 26.9 percent of the pages that did not have defined headings. There is 34.6 percent of the IITRLW that has been using Tables for layout in various places. The IITRLW has a WIF score of 1.90, an RWIF score of 0.94 and an OWIF score of 0.97 respectively.

The Composite Rank is calculated by adding WI, WATS, WIF, RWIF and OWIF scores and then dividing them with five to get the mean score where the WI score is 78 out of 105, WATS is 119.4 out of 260, WIF score is 1.90, RWIF score is 0.94 and OWIF score is 0.97. The total score from all five evaluative techniques is 201.2 and the mean score is 40.2. The Composite Rank is 11 and the Institutional Rank is 7.

4.3.8. IIT Guwahati Library Website (IITGLW)

Out of 105 web indicators, 64 (61 percent) are available and 41 (39 percent) are missing from IITGLW. The Information Block has scored the highest score i.e. 70 percent. It includes contact information of the library, campus sitemap, library staff directory, etc. while the floor plan of the library, web master contact details, visitor's number count, etc. are missing. The second highest score is obtained by the Design & Graphics Block with 66.66 percent. It is comprised of memorable URL, hyperlinks identity, etc. The homepage length is within one screenful of information while the multilingual access option, etc. are missing from IITGLW. The Links Block with 62.5

percent includes the link to parent institution's homepage, web directories, etc. However, free internet resources, the links to information manual, etc. are missing from the IITGLW. The Resource Block with the score of 50 percent, includes e-databases, e-books, e-journals, course materials, referencing tools, etc. whereas the new arrival list, library podcast, online reference chat, newspaper clippings, etc. are missing from IITGLW. The last position among the 5 blocks is held by the Service Block with 22.22 percent. It included OPAC, email reference of the librarian, etc. but lacked in the inter-library loan, online feedback, virtual users training session, digital communication forums, etc. Out of 26 tests, the IITGLW has scored the highest in 12 tests like the domain age, freshness, error pages, etc. It has an average score in 3 tests like popularity, incoming links and the amount of content. It scored low in 12 tests and these were Facebook, printability, W3C Compliance, etc. The score out of 260 is 126.6 (48.69 percent). There were 27 pages of IITGLW which were tested on 24th January 2017. The IITGLW written using HTML had 49 internal and 49 external broken links which were witnessed out of 1555 links tested by the Sitebeam. The average pages of the IITGLW take 2.7 seconds to download and 0.5 seconds to upload. There is 18.5 percent of the IITGLW which is using Tables for layouts and 96.3 percent of the pages use external stylesheets. On an average the IITGLW is updated after 2.3 weeks. The domain age is 13.4 years and the expiry date is 31/08/2019. IITGLW is optimized for mobile and tablet devices via 'responsive' designs. It does not use any recognized analytic software. It has neither a Facebook nor a Twitter account. There are 85.2 percent of the pages that are not using any defined headings. The IITGLW is not optimized for printing. It is W3C Compliant. The IITGLW have 868 potential spelling errors. Very few pages of the IITGLW are there on the search engine results. It was observed that 70.7 percent of the images on the IITGLW do not have alternative text.

The IITGLW does not use any Open Graph tag. There were 647 sites which were linked to the IITGLW. There are also three missing files in three pages. The IITGLW has not used even the Content Management System. The IITGLW has a WIF score of 0.032, RWIF score of 0.006 and OWIF score of 0.032.

The Composite Rank of IITGLW is calculated by adding WI, WATS, WIF, RWIF and OWIF and then dividing them with five to get the mean score where the WI score is 64 out of 105, WATS is 126.6 out of 260, the WIF score is 0.032 the RWIF score is 0.006 and the OWIF score is 0.032. Thus, the total score of all the five evaluative techniques is 190.7 and the mean score is 38.1. The Composite Rank is 14 and the Institutional Rank is 8.

4.3.9. NIT Rourkela Library Website (NITRLW)

Out of the total 105 web indicators, 68 (65 percent) were available and 37 (35 percent) were missing from the NITRLW. The Links Block scored the highest with 87.5 percent. It included the links to study program sites, the link to parent institution's homepage, links to information manuals, etc. while links to popular internet search engines and web directories were not present on the NITRLW. The second highest score was of the Information Block i.e. 80 percent. It contained the mission statement, floor plan, the short bibliographies of the staff, etc. but what was missing was the site map and web masters contact details. The Resource Block had 57.14 percent and included the availability of e-databases, e-books, e-journals, dictionaries, encyclopaedias, course materials and so on. The NITRLW lacks in tutorials on library related topics, subject bibliographies and directories, library glossary, etc. The Service Block scored the least i.e. 55.55 percent. It contained feasibility of OPAC; inter library loan, online feedback, online book reservation, email reference of the librarian and document delivery service, etc. However, virtual users training sessions, online orientation session, digital communication forum, etc. are not present on the NITRLW. The Design & Graphics scored 54.23 percent and was equipped with memorable URL, consistency in NITRLW layout, etc. The homepage length remained within one screenful of information and consistent navigation and so on were absent in the NITRLW. Out of 26 tests the NITRKLW scored the highest in 16 tests namely alternative text; amount of content, analytics, etc. It had an average score in 3 tests like incoming links, search engine results and social interest. It scored low in 7 tests and these were broken links, W3C Compliance, Facebook, etc. The total score out of 260 was 159 (61.15 percent). There were 100 pages of the NITRKLW which were tested on 3rd February 2017. There were 06 internal and 123 external links. It takes 14.1 seconds to download and 1 second per page to upload. No page of the NITRKLW is W3C Compliant. It was observed that 93 percent pages of the NITRKLW are written in HTML5. However, the NITRKLW has 2311 potential spelling errors. It has a Twitter account with 14 followers and three pages of NITRKLW are shared on Facebook. Only some of the pages in the NITRKLW appear in the search engine results. It does not use any Open Graph tags, although some basic information can be inferred from other tags. Also 10 other websites are linked to NITRKLW. There are 12 missing files which are spread over 9 pages. There are 6.6 percent of the images that do not have an alternative text. There were 53 percent of the NITRKLW which is using Google Analytics. Also 14 percent of the pages are not using well defined headings. There is 86 percent of the NITRKLW which is optimized for printing. The NITRKLW is updated every 1.3 weeks. There are 4 percent Tables used for layout of the NITRKLW. Also 96 percent of its pages are using external stylesheets. The NITRKLW is optimized for mobile and tablet devices via 'responsive' design. The NITRKLW is using the Joomla Content Management System. The NITRLW has a WIF score as 1.04, a RWIF score as 0.70 and an OWIF score as 0.33 respectively.

The Composite Rank is calculated by adding the scores of WI, WATS, WIF, RWIF and OWIF and then dividing them by five to get the mean score where the WI score is 68 out of 105, WATS is 159 out of 260, the WIF score is 1.040 the RWIF score is 0.70 and the OWIF score is 0.33. Therefore, the total score of all the five evaluative techniques is 229.1 and the mean score is 45.8. The Composite Rank is 3 and the Institutional Rank is 9.

4.3.10. Jawaharlal Nehru Centre for Advanced Scientific Research Library Website (JNCASRLW)

Out of the total 105 web indicators, 44 (42 percent) were available and 61 (58 percent) were missing from the JNCASRLW. The Design & Graphics Block scored the highest with 50 percent. It included memorable URL; website is consistent in layout, etc. though date of the last JNCASCRLW update, using heading tags, etc. are missing from JNCASRLW. The second position is secured by the Service Block with 44.44 percent score. It contains OPAC, document delivery service, inter-library loan, email reference of the librarian, etc. though online feedback, online book reservation, virtual users training session, digital communication forums were not included in JNCASRLW. The following block is the Information Block with a 40 percent score. It included the web masters contact details, short bibliographies of the staff members, library policies, library history, etc. whereas the mission statement and floor plan of the library, campus sitemap, photographs of staff members, frequently used sites, etc. are missing in the JNCASRLW. The next block is the Links Block with 25 percent. It contains free internet resources, links to OPAC of other libraries, etc. while links to study program sites, links to information manuals, etc. are missing from the JNCASRLW. The last position among the 5 blocks is of the Resource Block with 21.42 percent. It includes e-databases, e-books, e-journals, new arrival lists, course materials, etc. although the tutorials on library related topics, dictionaries and encyclopaedias, subject bibliographies, referencing tools are observed to be missing. Out of 26 tests, the JNCASRLW scored the highest in 11 tests namely domain age, freshness, error pages, etc. It has scored average in 5 tests like incoming links, Twitter, Facebook, etc. It has scored low in 10 tests which are broken links, missing files, analytics, etc. The score out of 260 is 137.7 (52.96 percent). The 100 pages of the JNCASRLW were tested on 24th January 2017. Eleven internal and 44 external links were found broken out of the 981 links tested by Sitebeam. There are 475 other websites linked to the JNCASRLW. It also has a Twitter account with 183 followers and a Facebook account with 1470 followers. Only 12 pages of the JNCASCRLW are shared on Facebook. The JNCASRLW takes 4.3 seconds to download and 0.6 seconds to upload a page. It is updated after every 3.9 weeks. While 5 percent pages of JNCASRLW are using tables for layout and 95 percent of JNCASRLW pages use Cascading Style Sheets. There is 85 percent of the JNCASRLW which is using the external stylesheets. The domain age is 13.9 years with the expiry date of 28/02/19. The JNCASRLW is optimized for mobile and tablet devices via 'responsive' design. The JNCASRLW is using the Word Press Content Management System. The JNCASRLW is not, however, using any recognized analytic software. There were 45 missing files spread over 13 pages. There is 4 percent of JNCASRLW which is optimized for printing. There are 98 percent of the pages that are W3C Compliant. It was seen that 49 percent of JNCASRLW was written using HTML4 and 37 percent was written using unspecified HTML while 9 percent was using XHTLM1 and 5 percent used HTML5. There were 1293 potential spelling errors on JNCASRLW. Very few pages in JNCASRLW are compatible with the search engine results but it is not using any Open Graph tags and 40 percent of the pages are not using well defined headings. There were 76.1 percent of the images that did not have alternative text. The JNCASCRLW has a WIF score of 1.677, RWIF score of 0.071 and an OWIF score of 1.609 respectively.

The Composite Rank is calculated by adding WI, WATS, WIF, RWIF and OWIF scores and then dividing them with five to get the mean score where the WI score is 44 out of 105, the WATS score is 137.7 out of 260 and the WIF score is 1.67, the RWIF score is 0.071 and the OWIF score is 1.609. Thus, the total score of all the five evaluative techniques is 185.1 and the mean score is 37.0. The Composite Rank is 19 and the Institutional Rank is 10.

4.3.11. NIT Trichy Library Website (NITTLW)

NIT Trichy Library Website (NITTLW) had 51 (48 percent) web indicators available out of a total of 105 while 54 (52 percent) were missing. The Design & Graphics Block scored the highest with 64.81 percent and included consistency in layout, date of last update, etc. while memorable URL, hyperlinks identity, etc. were missing. The Information Block was second with 45 percent and includes web indicators like mission statement, short bibliographies of the staff members, contact information, etc. while the floor plans, campus sitemap, etc. were missing. The third position was held by the Links Block with 37.5 percent as it contained the links to the parent institution's homepage, links to OPAC of other libraries, etc. but links to information manuals like library brochure, links to download necessary software tools, etc. were not included. The Service Block had 33.33 percent score and included OPAC, inter-library loan, email reference of the librarian, etc. but did not have online feedback, online book reservation, virtual users training session, etc. The last position among the 5 blocks was held by the Resource

Block with 7.14 percent score. It contained e-databases, e-books, e-journals, etc. while the tutorials on library related topics, library podcast, providing online reference chat, etc. which were missing on the NITTLW. It scored the highest in 9 tests namely domain age, error pages, analytics, etc. and scored averagely in 7 tests of freshness, incoming links, etc. It scored low in 10 tests and these were Facebook; missing files, Open Graphs, etc. The score out of 260 was 132.7 (51.04 percent). These 56 pages of the NITTLW have been tested on 24th January 2017. Out of the 204 links tested by Sitebeam 11 external links were broken and 593 other websites were linked to NITTLW. On average pages take 4.3 seconds to download and 0.4 seconds to upload. The NITTLW is updated every 5 months. Every page is using Google Analytics. The domain age of NITTLW is 13.5 years. All pages are using proper headings and it is optimized for mobile and tablet devices via 'responsive' design. The NITTLW has no Twitter account although two of its pages are shared on Facebook. There are 64 missing files over 56 pages and none of the pages are optimized. There are 722 spelling errors while none of the pages are W3C Compliant. Also very few pages appear in search engine results. 63.6 percent of the images do not have alternative text. It is not using any Content Management System. The WIF score is 2, RWIF score is 1 and OWIF score is 1.

The Composite Rank is calculated by adding WI, WATS, WIF, RWIF and OWIF scores and dividing them by five to get the mean score where the WI score is 51 out of 105, the WATS score is 132.7 out of 260 and the WIF score is 2, with the RWIF score being 1 and the OWIF score also being 1. The total score therefore, of all the five evaluative techniques is 187.7 and the mean score is 37.5. The Composite Rank is 17 and the Institutional Rank is 11.

4.3.12. BITS Pillani Library Website (BITPLW)

Out of the total 105 Web Indicators there were 58 (55 percent) which were available and 47 (45 percent) were missing from BITSPLW. The highest score was obtained by the Design & Graphics Block having 62.9 percent. It included memorable URL. The BITPLW is consistent in layout, avoids use of flash animation, etc., but it does provide multilingual access options, print friendly function, etc. The Information Block scored second highest with 60 percent. It included a floor plan of the BITPLW and availability of opening hours while web masters contact details, visitor's number count, etc. were not available. The Links Block was next with 50 percent. It included links to OPAC of other libraries, free internet resources of general interest, etc. while the links to study program sites, the links to download necessary software tool, etc. are missing. The Service Block secured 44.4 percent. It contained inter library loan, online book reservation, email reference of the librarian, etc. However document delivery service, virtual users training session; online feedback, etc. were missing. The last position was held by Resource Block with a score of 28.57 percent. It included e-databases, dictionaries and encyclopaedias, subject bibliographies, etc. however, it lacked in the tutorial on library related topics, referencing tools, course material, etc. Out of a total of the 26 tests, the BITPLW scored the highest in 13 tests which included the amount of content, domain age, alternative text, etc. It scored an average score in 4 tests like Facebook, URL format, popularity, etc. but its lowest score was in 9 tests namely analytics, broken links, etc. The score out of 260 is 147.9 (56.88 percent). While 100 pages of BITPLW were tested on 24th January 2017 it was observed that it had a Facebook account with 11,514 followers and a Twitter account with 10, 243 followers. On an average, the pages take 8.2 seconds to download and 1.2 seconds to upload. The BITPLW had 874 potential spelling errors and 703 other websites were linked to it. Only 2 missing files spread over 2 pages were cbserved. The website is updated every week. A very small number 0.6 percent of images do not have alternative text. The domain age is 13.9 years and the expiry date is 28/02/19. All pages has well defined headings. The BITPLW does not use any recognized analytics software. There are 101 internal and 04 external broken links out of the 811 links tested by Sitebeam. Very few pages of BITPLW are compatible with search engine results. All pages are W3C Compliant. It is not optimized for mobile or tablet devices. BITPLW does not use any Open Graph tags, while some basic information can be inferred from other tags. The BITPLW has neither used any Content Management System nor has it been optimized for printing. BITPLW has a WIF score of 0.033, RWIF score of 0.0004 and an OWIF score of 0.033.

The Composite Rank is calculated by adding WI, WATS, WIF, RWIF and OWIF and then dividing them by five to get the mean score where WI score is 58 out of 105, WATS is 147.9 out of 260, WIF score is 0.0331, RWIF score is 0.0004 and OWIF score is 0.033. Thus, the total score of all the five evaluative techniques is 206.0 and the mean score is 41.2. The Composite Rank is 10 and the Institutional Rank is 12.

4.3.13. International Institute of Information Technology, Hyderabad (IIITHLW)

Out of 105 web indicators, 39 (37 percent) were available and 66 (63 percent) were missing on the IIITHLW. The Design & Graphics Block scored high with 53.70 percent. It includes memorable URL; website is consistent in layout, etc. while date of the last update, use of high contrast of text and backgrounds, etc. are missing. The Links Block and Information Block were second. Both have possessed an equal score of 25 percent. The Links Block included links to the parent institution's homepage, free internet resources, etc. although links to study program sites, links to information manuals, etc. were missing. The Information Block included photographs of staff members, library staff directory, etc. but the mission statement, etc. were missing. Block was next with a score of 14.2 percent. It included dictionaries and encyclopaedias, bibliographies etc. though e-databases, e-books, e-journals, online reference chat, etc. were absent from the IIITHLW. The last position among the 5 blocks was held by the Service Block with a 11.11 percent score. It included inter library loan, document delivery service, etc. while digital communication forums, online orientation session, etc. were missing. Out of a total of 26 tests, the IIITHLW scored the highest in 10 tests namely alternative text, the amount of content, domain age, etc. It had an average score in 5 tests like broken links, incoming links, popularity, speed, etc. It scored low in 11 tests and these pertained to analytics, W3C Compliance, Facebook, etc. The score out of 260 was 141.5 (54.42 percent). A total of 100 pages of the IIITHLW have been tested on 24th January 2017. IIITHLW is not using any recognized analytic software. The IIITHLW does not have a Twitter account but one page is shared on Facebook with 71 followers. There were 96 missing files spread over 95 pages. Also 90 percent of the pages were not W3C Compliant. The IIITHLW has 1703 potential spelling errors. It does not use any Open Graph tags. Very few pages of the IIITHLW are compatible in search engine results. There were 04 internal and 16 external broken links out of the total 860 links tested by Sitebeam. The IIITHLW takes 3.7 seconds to download and 0.3 seconds per page to upload. The frequency of updating the IIITHLW is 2.8 months. There were 11.3 percent of the images that do not have alternative text. Also 2 percent of the pages do not have defined headings. There was 98 percent of the IIITHLW which optimized for printing. Also 1 percent of the IIITHLW was using Tables for layout. The domain age is 12.6 years and the expiry date is 26/06/24. The IIITHLW has been optimized for mobile and tablet devices via 'responsive' design. The IIITHLW was not using any Content Management System. The IIITHLW has a WIF score of 0.0086, the RWIF score of 0.004 and an OWIF score of 0.0086 is observed.

The Composite Rank is calculated by adding the WI, WATS, WIF, RWIF and OWIF scores and dividing them by five to obtain the mean score where the WI score is 39 out of 105, the WATS is 141.5 out of 260. Also the WIF score is 0.086, the RWIF score is 0.0004 and the OWIF score is 0.0086. Thus, the total score of all the five evaluative techniques is 180.5 and the mean score is 36.1. The Composite Rank is 23 and the Institutional Rank is 13.

4.3.14. NIT Calicut Library Website (NITCLW)

Out of the total 105 web indicators, 50 (48 percent) were available and 55 (52 percent) were missing from NITCLW. The Design & Graphics Block scored the highest with 64.81 percent. It included the homepage and the length is within one screenful of information; memorable URL, etc. however, hyperlinks identities, multilingual access options, etc. are missing. The second highest score was obtained by the Information Block having 45 percent. It comprised contact information of the library, availability of opening hours, etc. However, the mission statement and the floor plan of the library, web masters contact details etc. were missing. The third position was held by the Links Block with 37.5 percent. It included links to parent institution's homepage, etc. whereas the links to study program sites, the links to download necessary software tool, etc. were not included. The next block is the Service Block with a score of 22.22 percent. It includes OPAC, email reference of the librarian, etc. however, inter library loan, online feedback, online book reservation, virtual users training session, etc. were missing. At the last position is the Resource Block with 7.14 percent score. It contains e-databases, e-books, e-journals, etc. while tutorials on library related topics, directories, course materials, referencing tools, etc. were all missing. Out of the total 26 tests, the NITCLW has scored the highest in 12 tests like domain age, error pages, the amount of content, etc. It had an average score in only 1 test i.e. broken links but it scored low in 13 tests and these included Facebook, alternative text, headings, etc. The score out of a total of 260 is 128.1 (49.26 percent). In all 44 pages of the NITCLW were tested on 24th January 2017. There were 98 percent pages of NITCLW were written in HTML5 and 2 percent pages were written in unspecified HTML. The domain age of the NITCLW is 12.6 years and the expiry date is 30/06/24. NITCLW is updated every 2.3 weeks. The NITCLW has no Twitter account but shared two pages on Facebook. There were 86.4 percent of the pages with no defined headings. NITCLW is optimized for printing.Very few pages in NITCLW are compatible with search engine results. There are 4.55 percent of Google Analytics users with 93.2 percent of the pages being non W3C Compliant. The site is not using any Open Graph tags, although some basic information can be inferred from other tags. It is not optimized for mobile or tablet devices. There were 5 websites linked to NITCLW. Also 63.8 percent of the images do not have alternative text. Only 01 internal and 38 external broken links out of 5853 links have been tested by Sitebeam. On an average, the pages took two seconds to download and 0.3 seconds per page to upload. There were 02 missing files are spread over 02 pages. There was 2.3 percent of the NITCLW using Tables of layout and 97.7 percent pages used external stylesheets. It does not use any Content Management System. The NITCLW has a WIF score of 4.91, RWIF of 2.03 and as OWIF score of 1.33 respectively.

The Composite Rank is calculated by adding WI, WATS, WIF, RWIF and OWIF. Then it is divided by five to get the mean score where the WI score is 50 out of 105, WATS is 128.1 out of 260, and the WIF score is 3.362, with RWIF score being 2.034 and the OWIF score being 1.328. Thus, the total score of all the five evaluative techniques is 184.8 and the mean score is 37. The Composite Rank is 21 and the Institutional Rank is 15.

4.3.15. The Institute of Mathematical Sciences Library Website (IMSCLW)

From among the total 105 Web Indicators, 54 (52 percent) were available and 51 (48 percent) were missing. The Information Block scored the highest which was 60 percent. It included the floor plan, site map, contact information, etc. But the Vision and Mission Statements, web masters contact details; library policies, etc. were all missing. The Design & Graphics Block secured 57.4 percent and took the second highest position. It included memorable URL, hyperlinks identity and avoidance of horizontal scrolling, however, date of last website update, avoidance of use of flash animation were missing from the IMSCLW. The Service Block secured 55.55 percent score and was composed of OPAC, inter library loan service, online book reservation, email reference of the librarian, etc. but it lacked virtual users training session, document delivery service, digital communication forums, etc. The fourth position was secured by the Links Block with 37.5 percent score. It contained free internet resources, OPAC of other libraries, etc. though the links to study program sites, the links to information manuals and the links to popular search engines were missing. The last position was obtained by the Resource Block with 21.42 percent. It included e-databases, e-books, e-journals, subject bibliographies, directories, referencing tools, etc. while the tutorials on library related topics, dictionaries and encyclopaedias, library podcasts, new arrival list, etc. were not included. Out of a total of 26 tests, the IMSCLW scored highest in 13 tests like the amount of content, alternative text, domain age, etc. It had an average score in 5 tests namely popularity, social internet, incoming links, etc. It scored low in 8 tests and these were Facebook, broken links, analytics, etc. The score out of 260 was 149.7 (57.57 percent). A total of 100 pages of the IMSCLW were tested on 3rd February 2017. It was observed that 33 internal and 16 external links were broken out of the total 1086 links tested by Sitebeam. There were 747 websites linked to IMSCLW. On an average the pages took 4.1 seconds to download and 0.3 seconds to upload. There were 5 missing files spread over 4 pages. Only two percent of the pages were not using proper headings. There were 98 percent of the IMSCLW pages which used external stylesheets. Only 0.1 percent of the images do not have alternative text. The domain age of the IMSCLW is 12.7 years and the expiry date is 30/04/24. The IMSCLW is updated daily. It has been optimized for mobile and tablet devices via 'responsive' design. It has been using the Drupal Content Management System but it is not using any recognized analytics software. It has no Twitter account but 20 percent of the IMSCLW is shared on Facebook. Only two percent of IMSCLW is optimized for printing. There were 2064 potential spelling errors. Also 98 percent of the pages are W3C Compliant. There is 95 percent of the IMSCLW written using XHTML1 and 5 percent is written using unspecified HTML. Very few pages in IMSCLW are compatible with search engine results and it is not using Open Graph tags. The IMSCLW has a WIF score as 2.16, RWIF score of 0.04 and an OWIF score of 2.11.

The Composite Rank is calculated by adding WI, WATS, WIF, RWIF and OWIF and then dividing the result by 5 to get the mean score where WI score is 54 out of 105, WATS is 149.7 out of 260, the WIF score is 2.16, the RWIF score is 0.04 and the OWIF score is 2.11. Therefore, the total score of all five evaluative techniques is 208 and the mean score is 41.6. The Composite Rank is 8 and the Institutional Rank is 16.

4.3.16. Indian Agricultural Research Institute Library Website (IARILW)

From among the total 105 web indicators, 48 (46 percent) are available and 57 (54 percent) are missing from the IARILW. The Design & Graphics Block scored the highest with 66.66 percent. It included memorable URL, accessed the home page from all other pages, etc. but the homepage length is within one screenful of information and the date of the last IARILW update, etc. were missing. The second highest score was of the Links Block at 37.5 percent. It was composed of links to parent institution's homepage, etc. but the links to information manuals like library brochure, etc. are missing. At the third position was the Service Block with 33.33 percent. It comprised the availability of OPAC, inter library loan, online feedback, etc. however, the online book reservations, email reference of the librarian, virtual users training session, document delivery service and digital communication forums were not included. The Information Block had scored 20 percent and consisted of the institution's name, contact information, copyright statement, etc. but mission statement was missing. The last position among the 5 blocks belonged to the Resource Block with 14.28 percent. It included research publication of academic staff, new arrivals lists, etc. however, the tutorials on library related topics, dictionaries, encyclopaedias, etc. were missing. Out of a total of 26 tests the IARILW scored the highest in 11 tests namely freshness, headings, error pages, etc. It scored an average score in 4 tests like broken links, incoming links, alternative text, etc. It scored low in 11 tests and these were W3C Compliance, missing files, mobile, etc. The score out of a total of 260 was 135.2 (52 percent). All of 100 pages of IARILW were tested on 24th January 2017. All pages of the IARILW were written using HTML5. And 02 internal and 07 external broken links were found out of the 537 links tested. The IARILW is updated after every 7 days on an average. The domain age is 14.3 years and the expiry date is 25/10/18. All pages have well defined headings. The IARILW is also optimized for printing and it used Joomla Content Management System. It does not use any recognized analytic software. Only one page in the IARILW is shared on Facebook with 31 followers and has no Twitter account. There are 4201 spelling errors in the IARILW. It is W3C Compliant and is not optimized for mobile and tablet devices. On an average one page take 6.9 seconds to download and 0.9 seconds per page to upload. Very few pages of the IARILW were traced in a search engines results. There were 51.4 percent of images that did not have any alternative text and is not using any Open Graph tags. There were 415 other websites linked to the IARILW.

The Composite Rank is calculated by adding WI, WATS, WIF, RWIF and OWIF and then dividing the result by 5 to get the mean score. The IARILW has a WIF score of two an RWIF score of one and an OWIF score of one. Therefore, the total score of all the five evaluative techniques is 187.2 and the mean score is 37.4. Both Composite and Institutional Rank is 18.

4.3.17. IIT Hyderabad Library Website (IITHLW)

From among the total 105 web indicators, 43 (41 percent) were available and 62 (59 percent) were missing from the IITHLW. The Design & Graphics Block scored the highest with 57.4 percent. It included memorable URL, hyperlinks identity, provide last date of IITHLW update, etc., but did not have web indicators like homepage length which is within one screenful of information, written abbreviations and acronyms fully in the first instance, etc. The second position belonged to the Links Block with 37.5 percent. It comprised links to parent institution's homepage, free internet resources of general interest, links to OPAC of related libraries, etc. while the links to study program sites, etc. were missing. The Information Block was next with 30 percent score. It included mission statement, short bibliographies and photographs of staff members, etc. but did not have the floor plan, campus sitemap, web masters contact details, visitor's number, etc. The Resource Block had 14.28 percent score. It contained dictionaries and encyclopaedias, referencing tools, etc but did not have e-databases, e-books, e-journals, subject bibliographies, library podcast, online reference chat, etc. The last position in all the 5 blocks was the Service Block with 11.11 percent scores. It included email reference of the librarian, etc. but did not have OPAC, inter library loan, online feedback, online book reservation, document delivery service; digital communication forums, etc. Out of the total 26 tests, IITHLW scored the highest in 13 tests like domain age, alternative text, analytics, etc. It had an average score in two tests namely incoming links, readability; etc. It had a low score in 11 tests and these were search engine results, social interest, W3C Compliance, etc. The score out of 260 is 141.1 (54.26 percent). A total of 89 pages of the IITHLW were tested on 24th January 2017. The IITHLW does not use any recognized analytic software. The IITHLW has a Facebook account with 71 followers but does not have a Twitter account. There are 96 missing files which are spread over 95 pages. There are 99 percent of the pages which are not W3C Compliant. Also, 98 percent of IITHLW is written using XHTML1 but there are 1703 spelling errors and it is not optimized for mobile or tablet devices. It does not use any Open Graph tags. There are very few pages of the IITHLW which are traced in the search engine results. There are 04 internal and 19 external broken links among 860 links that were tested. On an average the pages take 3.7 seconds to download and 0.3 seconds per page to upload. The IITHLW is updated after every 2.8 months. There are 11.3 percent of the images that do not have the alternative text specified. Only 0.2 percent of the pages do not have well defined headings. Also 98 percent was optimized for printing. One percent of the IITHLW used Tables for layout. Almost all pages used external stylesheets. The domain age is 12.6 years and the expiry date is 26/06/24. No Content Management System is being used. The IITHLW has a WIF score of 2.043 the RWIF score of 0.976 and the OWIF score of 1.068.

The Composite Rank is calculated by adding WI, WATS, WIF, RWIF and OWIF and dividing the score by five to get a mean score where the WI score is 43 out of 105 the WATS score is 141.1 out of 260 and the WIF score is 2.04, RWIF score is 0.97 and the OWIF score is 1.06. Thus, the total score of all the five evaluative techniques is 188.2 and the mean score is 37.6. The Composite Rank is 16 and the Institutional Rank is 19.

4.3.18. ISB Hyderabad Library Website (ISBHLW)

Out of a total of 105 web indicators, 55 (52 percent) was available and 50 (48 percent) was missing from the ISBHLW. The Design & Graphics Block scored the highest position with 62.29 percent. It is comprised of memorable URL, avoiding the use of flash animation, etc. However, written abbreviations and acronyms, etc. were missing indicators from ISBHLW. The Service Block scored second highest position with 55.55 percent. It had OPAC, inter library loan, online reservation, email reference of the librarian, document delivery service, etc. but did not have online feedback, digital communication forum, etc. The Information Block was next with 45 percent. It included library policies, institutions full name, FAQs, etc. but did not have webmaster contact details, short biographies of the staff members, etc. The Links Block with 37.5 percent contained free internet resources of general interest, the links to OPAC of other libraries, etc. but did not have the links to the study sites, the links to information manuals, etc. The Resource Block had 28.57 percent and included e-data base, e-books, e-journals, dictionaries and encyclopaedias while subject bibliographies and referencing tools were excluded from ISBHLW. Out of a total 26 tests the ISBHLW scored the highest on 16 tests namely Twitter, stylesheets, typosquatting, etc. It scored less than average on four tests like incoming links, readability, etc. It had a low score on 6 tests and these printability, spelling, etc. The total score out of 260 was 187.5 (72.11 percent). A total of 100 pages of the ISBHLW were tested on 24th January 2017. The ISBHLW is not optimized for printing but had 1735 potential spelling errors. All the pages are W3C Compliant. All pages of the ISBHLW were written in XHTML1. Very few pages of ISBHLW could be traced in search engine results. The site did not use any Open Graph tags, although some basic information could be inferred from other tags. There were 945 other websites linked to the ISBHLW. No internal broken links existed but 07 external broken links were observed from 726 links tested. The ISBHLW has a Facebook page with 128,901 followers and a Twitter account with 137,904 followers. It takes 1.3 seconds to download and 0.2 seconds to upload a page. On an average the ISBHLW is updated every 3 days and all pages use Google Analytics. The domain age is 16.2 years but the expiry date is unknown. All pages have well defined headings. It is optimized for mobile and tablet devices via 'responsive' design. The ISBHLW is using the Drupal Content Management System. The ISBHLW has a WIF score of 1.783, an RWIF score of 0.767 and an OWIF score of 1.016.

The Composite Rank is calculated by adding WI, WATS, WIF, RWIF and OWIF and then dividing the total score by five to get the mean score where WI score is 55 out of 105, WATS is 187.5 out of 260, WIF is 1.78, RWIF score is 0.76 and the OWIF score is 1.01. Thus, the total score of all the five evaluative techniques is 246.1 and the mean score is 49.2. The Composite Rank is 1 and the Institutional Rank is 20.

4.3.19. IIM Ahmedabad Library Website (IIMALW)

Among the total 105 web indicators the IIMALW had available web indicators as 68 (65 percent) and 37 (35 percent) web indicators as missing. The Link Block included the link to parent institution's homepage, the links to free internet resources, etc. but did not include the links to information manuals, popular search engines, etc. The Information Block included short bibliographies and photographs of staff, help guides, but lacked the Mission Statement, frequently used sites, visitors count, etc. The Design and Graphics Block scored 66.66 percent. It was comprised of memorable URL; IIMALW is consistent in layout, etc. However, date of the last IIMALW update; multilingual access options, etc. were missing. The next block is the Service Block i.e. 55.55 percent. It provided OPAC, inter library loan, online book reservation, document delivery service while online feedback, virtual training sessions, digital communication forums, etc. were missing. The Resource Block scored 42.85 percent. It included e-data bases, dictionaries, referencing tools, library glossary, etc. and yet did not include the tutorial on library related topics, library podcast, online reference chat, etc. Out of a total of 26 tests the IIMALW scored the highest in nine tests like freshness, domain age, error pages, etc. It had an average score in three tests namely missing files, Open Graph, popularity, etc. It had a low score in 14 tests and these are spelling, search engine results, etc. The score out of a total of 260 was 123.5 (47.5 percent). A total of 100 pages of IIMALW were tested on 24th January 2017. The IIMALW had 127 internal and 32 external links, out of the total 1053 links tested. The majority of the IIMALW i.e. 99 percent of the pages was not using proper headings and is not optimized for printing. Very few pages of the IIMALW traced in the search engine results. No pages were W3C Compliant. Only 88 percent of the IIMALW was written using XHTML1. The

IIMALW had 1389 potential spelling errors. It has a Twitter account with 20 followers while the Facebook account has 2055 followers. There are 71.9 percent of images which have not been optimized for mobile or tablet devices. Only four other websites are linked to the IIMALW. It is not using any Open Graph tags. There were 25 missing files over two pages. On an average the pages take 1.0 seconds to download and 0.1 seconds to upload. Nearly 88 percent of the IIMALW is using Google Analytics software. It is updated every 4.8 days. Only two percent of the IIMALW used Tables for layout. Also 98 percent of the IIMALW used Cascading Style Sheet. There were 88 percent that used external sytlesheets. The domain age is 9 years. The expiry date is 14/02/20. It is using the Drupal Content Management System. The IIMALW has a WIF score of 1.04, an RWIF score of 0.04 and an OWIF score of 0.57.

The Composite Rank is calculated by adding WI, WATS, WIF, RWIF and OWIF and then dividing the resultant score with five to get the mean score where the WI score is 68 out of 105, the WATS score is 123.5 out of 260, while the WIF score is 1.04, the RWIF score is 0.04 and the OWIF score is 0.57. The total score of all five evaluative techniques is 193.1 and the mean score is 38.6. The Composite Rank is 13 and the Institutional Rank is 21.

4.3.20. Indian Institutes of Science Education and Research Kolkata Library Website (IISERKLW)

Out of the 105 web indicators, 38 (36 percent) were available and 67 (64 percent) were missing from the IISERKLW. The Design & Graphics Block scored the highest with 59.25 percent. It included memorable URL consistence in layout, headlines that support scanning, etc. but did not include navigational aids, large graphics, providing multilingual access options, etc. The second highest score was obtained by the Links Block having a

25 percent score. It included link to parent institution's homepage, free internet resources, etc. though links to study program sites, links to download necessary software tool, link to information manual, etc. were missing. The Resource Block scored 14.2 percent and contained e-database, e-books, e-journals, directories, etc. However, the tutorials on library related topics, course materials, referencing tools, etc. were missing. The Service Block had a score of 11.11 percent. It involved online orientation sessions but OPAC, online book reservation, inter library loan, online feedback, etc. were missing. The last position among the 5 blocks belonged to the Information Block with a score of only 5 percent. It included full institutions name but did not include mission statement and the floor plan of the library, etc. Out of the 26 tests the IISERKLW scored the highest in 10 tests namely analytics, domain age, alternative text, etc. It had an average score in 7 tests like the amount of content, broken links, incoming links, freshness, etc. It had a low score in 9 tests and these are the Open Graph, Facebook, etc. The scores out of 260 were 146.6 (56.38 percent). A total of 16 pages were tested on 3rd February 2017. There were four missing files in three pages. Also 170 other websites were linked to the IISERKLW. It takes 4.5 seconds to download pages and 1.8 seconds to upload pages. There were 01 internal and 64 external broken links out of a total of 3545 links tested. Only 0.8 percent of the images did not have alternative text. All pages in the IISERKLW used Google Analytics. The domain age is 10.1 years and the expiry date is 12/01/18. All pages had defined headings. The IISERKLW used Joomla Content Management System. There were no Twitter and Facebook accounts in the IISERKLW. It is not optimized for printing. All the pages are W3C Compliant. The IISERKLW is not using any Open Graph tags and is not optimized for mobile and tablet devices. The IISERKLW had 1213 spelling errors. Very few pages were traced by the search engine. On an average

the IISERKLW is updated after every 20 months. The IISERKLW had a WIF score of 2.17, an RWIF score of 0.79 and an OWIF score of 1.38 respectively.

The Composite Rank is calculated by adding WI, WATS, WIF, RWIF and OWIF and then dividing the total with five to get the mean score where the WI score is 38 out of the 105, WATS is 146.6 out of 260, the WIF score is 2.17, the RWIF score is 0.79 and the OWIF score is 1.38. Therefore, the total score of all the five evaluative techniques is 189 and the mean score is 37.8. The Composite Rank is 15 and the Institutional Rank is 22.

4.3.21. IISER Pune Library Website (IISERPLW)

Out of a total of 105 web indicators, 59 (56 percent) are available and 46 (44 percent) are not. The Design & Graphics Block had the highest position with 66.66 percent. It included memorable URL, hyperlinks identity, date of last website update, etc. and did not include homepage length is within one screenful of information, etc. The second highest score was obtained by the Information Block with 60 percent. It included help guide and instructions, the floor plan, etc. but did not include visitor's number count, web masters contact details; campus sitemap, etc. The third position went to the Service Block with 55.55 percent. It included OPAC, inter library loan, online book reservation, email reference of the librarian etc. but online feedback, digital communication forums, etc. were not included. The next block is the Links Block with 37.5 percent. It included links to parent institution's homepage, links to OPAC of other libraries, etc. but on the other hand the links to information manuals, links to download necessary software tool, etc. were missing. The last position among the 5 blocks was the Resource Block with 21.42 percent. It included e-data bases, e-books, e-journals, subject bibliographies, research publications of academic staff, etc. but did not include the tutorials on library related topics, referencing tools, reading list recommended by faculty, etc. Out of 26 tests the IISERPLW scored the highest in 9 tests namely domain age, error pages, analytics etc. but had an average score in 6 tests like the amount of content, broken links, incoming links etc. It had a low score in 11 tests and these were alternative text, Facebook, headings, etc. The score out of a total 260 was 130.6 (50.2 percent). In all 23 pages of the IISERPLW were tested on 3rd February 2017. Of their pages 69.6 percent did not have proper headings. The IISERPLW is not optimized for printing and very few pages were traced clearly in search engine results. The ISERPLW had 750 potential spelling errors. It has no Twitter account but one of its pages is shared on Facebook. There are 76.2 percent of the images that do not have alternative text and have not been optimized for mobile and tablet devices. Also 293 other websites are linked to the ISERPLW. There were four internal and 44 external broken links out of the total 2084 links tested. On an average, pages take 3.9 seconds to download and 0.3 seconds per page to upload. There is 69 percent of the ISERPLW that uses Google Analytics software. ISERPLW is W3C Compliant. On an average, the site is updated every 1.2 months. The domain age is 10.7 years and the expiry date is 29/05/24. It does not use any Content Management System. The IISERPLW has a WIF score of 9.18, the RWIF score is 4.06 and the OWIF score is 5.12 respectively.

The Composite Rank is calculated by adding WI, WATS, WIF, RWIF and OWIF and then dividing the score obtained by five to get the mean score where the WI score is 59 out of 105, the WATS is 130.6 out of 260 and the WIF score is 9.18, the RWIF score is 4.06 and the OWIF score is 5.12. Thus, the total score of all the five evaluative techniques is 208.0 and the mean score is 41.6. The Composite Rank is 8 and the Institutional Rank is 23.

4.3.22. NIT Karnataka Library Website (NITKLW)

Among the 105 Web Indicators, 48 (46 percent) were available and 57 (54 percent) were missing from the NITKLW. The Information Block scored the highest with 60 percent and included the photographs of staff members, etc. but did not include the floor plan, campus sitemap, web masters contact details, visitor number count, etc. The Service Block with 55.55 percent included OPAC, inter library loan, email to reference of the librarian, document delivery service, etc. However, the online feedback, virtual users training session, digital communication forums and online orientation sessions were missing from the NITKLW. At the third position was the Design & Graphics Block with a score of 46.25 percent. It included memorable URL, accessing the home page from all other pages, etc. It did not include date of last website update, homepage length is within one screenful of information; etc. The Links Block with 37.5 percent was fourth and included the link to parent institution's homepage, free internet resources, the links to OPAC of other libraries but did not include the links to course and study program sites, links to download necessary software tool, etc. The last position among the 5 blocks was held by the Resource Block with 21.42 percent score. It contained e-databases, e-books, e-journals, etc. but did not contain the tutorials on library related topics, dictionaries and encyclopaedias, subject bibliographies, referencing tools, etc.

Out of the 26 tests, the NITKLW scored the highest in 9 tests namely stylesheets, typosquatting, URL format, etc. It had an average score in two tests like readability and the amount of content. It had a low score in 15 tests and these were alternative text, analytics, broken links, etc. The score out of 260 was 110.9 (42.65 percent). All 23 pages of the NITKLW were tested on 3rd February 2017.

The site does not use any recognized analytics software. Only one internal and 5 external links were broken out of the 96 tested. There were 90 percent of the pages that were not well defined headings. It was observed that 10 missing files were spread over 10 pages. The NITKLW is not optimized for printing and all pages were written in HTML5. There were 117 potential spelling errors on the NITKLW. It has no Twitter account but one page is shared on Facebook. There are 86.8 percent of the images that do not have alternative text. The NITKLW is not optimized for mobile and tablet devices. It is also not using any Open Graph tags although some basic information could be inferred from other tags. Very few pages in the NITKLW could be traced in the search engine results. Only two websites were linked to NITKLW, which was updated every two months. NITKLW is ranked 69,570th in the world for popularity by Alexa. The domain age is 14.5 years and the expiry date is 08/08/24. NITKLW is not using any Content Management System.

The NITKLW has a WIF score of 1.93, an RWIF score of 0.88 and an OWIF score of 1.04.

The Composite Rank is calculated by adding the five i.e., WI, WATS, WIF, RWIF and OWIF and dividing their score by five to get the mean score where the WIs score is 48 out of 105, the WATS is 110.9 out of 260, the WIF score is 1.93, the RWIF score is 0.88 and the OWIF score is 1.04. Thus, the total score of all the five evaluative techniques is 162.8 and the mean score is 32.6. The Composite Rank is 25 and the Institutional Rank is 24.

4.3.23. IIT Bhuvneshwar Library Website (IITBBSLW)

From among the 105 web indicators, 59 (56 percent) were available and 46 (44 percent) were not available. The Service Block had the highest position with 77.77 percent but it included the availability of OPAC, email reference of the librarian, document delivery service, etc.

but it did not include online feedback, virtual users training session, digital communication forums, etc. The second highest score was obtained by the Links Block with a score of 75 percent. It included the link to the parent institution's homepage, free internet resources, the links to download necessary software tools, etc. However the links to popular internet search engines, web directories, etc. were missing from the IITBBSLW. The Information Block with a score of 70 percent included the Vision and Mission Statements, library policies, help guide, etc. but did not include the visitor's number count, campus sitemap, staff with photographs, etc. The fourth position was held by the Design & Graphics Block with 61.11 percent and it included memorable URL, avoiding usage of background sounds, etc. but did not included the date of the last IITBBSLW update, multilingual access options, etc. The last position was obtained by the Resource Block with 21.42 percent. It included e-data bases, e-books, e-journals, new arrival lists, course material and did not include the tutorials on library related topics; referencing tools, subject bibliographies, etc. Out of 26 tests the IITBBSLW scored highest in 13 tests namely alternative text, the amount of content, domain age, etc. It has scored average level in 5 tests like error pages, missing files, freshness, etc. It scored low on 8 tests which included Facebook, analytics, incoming links etc. The score from 260 was 151.6 (58.30 percent). Total 100 pages of the IITBBSLW were tested on 3rd February 2017 not using any recognized analytics software. It has a Twitter account and four pages have also been shared on Facebook. The IITBBSLW is not W3C Compliant. All of 81 percent of IITBBSLW pages were written using HTML5 and another 19 percent of its pages were written using HTML. The IITBBSLW had 1906 potential spelling errors. Very few pages in the IITBBSLW were traced in search engine results. The IITBBSLW is not using any Open Graph tags although some basic information could be inferred from other tags. There were 5 websites linked to IITBBSLW. It had 2 internal and 54 external broken links out of the total 1751 tested links. The IITBBSLW is updated every 6 months and 18 percent of the pages of IITBBSLW were not using well-defined headings. On an average the pages took 2.7 seconds to download and 0.3 seconds per page to upload. The IITBBSLW is ranked 79699th in the world for popularity by Alexa. Also 18 percent of the website was using tables for layout. There were 81 percent of the pages of the IITBBSLW which used external stylesheets and 82 percent of the IITBBSLW used Cascading Style Sheet and is not using any Content Management System. The IITBBSLW is optimized for mobile and tablet devices via 'responsive' design. The domain age is 8.1 years. IITBBSLW has a WIF score of 1.77, an RWIF score 0.77 and an OWIF score 1.00.

The Composite Rank is calculated by adding WI, WATS, WIF, RWIF and OWIF and then dividing the sum by them with five to get the mean score where WI score is 59 out of 105, WATS is 151.6, out of 260 and WIF score is 1.77, RWIF score is 0.77 and OWIF score is 1. Thus, the total score of all five evaluative techniques is 214.1 and the mean score is 42.8. The Composite Rank is 6 and the Institutional Rank is 25.

4.3.24. Thapar University Library Website (THULW)

Out of the 105 web indicators, 59 (56 percent) were available and 46 (44 percent) were not available at this website. The Design & Graphics Block scored highest with 70.37 percent and includes hyperlinks identity, memorable URL, uses descriptive headings, etc. but it did not include date of last THULW update, provide multilingual access options, etc. The second highest score was obtained by Information Block with a score of 50 percent. It included help guides and instructions on the usage of library, the floor plan of the library, campus sitemap, etc. but did not include web masters contact details; FAQs, staff photographs, visitor's number count, etc. The next Service Block with 44.44 percent included inter library loan, email reference of the librarian, document delivery service, etc. but did not include virtual users training session, digital communication forums, etc. At the fourth position was the Links Block with a score of 37.5 percent and it contained the links to OPAC of other libraries, free internet resources of general interest, etc. but did not include the links to information manuals, the links to internet search engines, the links to related sites, etc. The last position belonged to the Resource Block with a score of 28.57 percent. It included e-databases, e-books, e-journals, etc. but did not include the tutorials on library related topics, library podcast, newspaper clippings, etc. Out of the 26 tests, THULW scored the highest in 11 tests like freshness, analytics, etc. It had only average scores in 7 tests like Facebook, alternative text, readability, etc. and it scored low in 8 tests which were Twitter, W3C Compliance, etc. The score from 260 is 154.9 (59.57 percent). Total 100 pages of the THULW were tested on 24th January 2017. It had no Twitter account but shared 7 pages on Facebook with 5262 followers. On an average the pages take 9.0 seconds to download and 2.1 seconds per page to upload. There were 189 websites linked to THULW. Only 04 external links were broken out of 1003 links tested. On an average the THULW is updated after every 1.9 weeks. Most headings of the THULW were well defined. Every page in THULW is using Google Analytics and it is optimized for mobile and tablet devices via 'responsive' design. It is using Joomla Content Management System. Only 8 percent of the THULW is optimized for printing. It had 2186 potential spelling errors. Very few pages in THULW could be traced in the search engine results. The THULW is neither using Open Graph tags nor is it W3C Compliant. There were 29.7 percent of the images that did not have alternative text. The WIF score of 1.81, the RWIF score of 0.82 and the OWIF score of 0.98 respectively.

The Composite Rank is calculated by adding WI, WATS, WIF, RWIF and OWIF and then dividing the sum by five to get the mean score where WI score is 59 out of

105, WATS is 154.9 out of 260, WIF score is 1.814, RWIF score is 0.82 and OWIF score is 0.98. Thus, the total score of all five evaluative techniques is 217.5 and the mean score is 43.5. The Composite Rank is 5 and the Institutional Rank is 14.

4.3.25. Saha Institute of Nuclear Physics Library Website (SINPLW)

Out of 105 web indicators, 52 (50 percent) were available and 53 (50 percent) were not. The Links Block scored the highest with 75 percent. It included the links to study program sites, free internet resources of general interest, the links to download necessary software tool, etc. but did not include links to information manuals, the links to popular internet search engines, etc. The Design & Graphics Block with 59.25 percent was composed of memorable URL, avoidance of horizontal scrolling, homepage length is within one screenful of information and date of last SINPLW update is not involved in SINPLW. The Information Block had third position with the score of 45 percent. It included institution's name, library history, etc. but the floor plan, campus sitemap, short biographies of staff members, etc. were not included. The Service Block had a 33.33 percent score and included OPAC, user online feedback, e-mail reference of the librarian whereas inter library loan, online book reservation, digital communication forum, etc. did not include in SINPLW. The last position was of Resource Block with a score of 21.42 percent. It contained e-databases, e-books, e-journals, newspaper clippings etc. but did not have tutorials on library related topics, subject bibliographies, directories, library podcast, online reference chat, etc. Out of 26 tests, SINPLW scored the highest in 11 tests like headings, domain age, freshness, etc. It scored average in two tests namely the amount of content, alternative text, etc. It scored low in 13 tests and these are Facebook, error pages, broken links, analytics, etc. The score from 260 is 128.9 (49.57 percent). A total of 100 pages of SINPLW were tested on 24th January 2017. It is not using any recognized analytics software. Two pages in SINPLW were shared on Facebook but SINPLW had no Twitter account. None of the pages of SINPLW were optimized for printing. SINPLW had 2011 spelling errors and 99 percent of the pages were not W3C Compliant. 96 percent of SINPLW is written using HTML5 whereas another 4 percent is written using unspecified HTML. Two internal and 30 external broken links were present out of 778 total links tested. On an average the pages took 7.7 seconds to download and 3.3 seconds per page to upload. The site is not using any Open Graph tags. There were 16 other websites that are linked to SINPLW. Also 59.2 percent of images did not have alternative text. It is ranked 283,785th in the world for popularity by Alexa. The SINPLW, on an average, was updated after every 2 months. There were 5 missing files which were spread over 3 pages. Only 3 percent of the pages were not using defined headings. The domain age is 7.3 years. One percent of the SINPLW was using Tables for layout. Ninety-nine percent of website used external stylesheets. It is optimized for mobile and tablet devices via 'responsive' design. The SINPLW is using Drupal and Word Press as Content Management System. The SINPLW has a WIF score of 1.4873, an RWIF score of 0.4873 and an OWIF score of 1.0 respectively.

The Composite Rank is calculated by adding WI, WATS, WIF, RWIF and OWIF and then dividing the sum by five to get the mean score where the WI score is 53 out of 105, WATS is 128.9 out of 260 and the WIF score is 1.4873, the RWIF score is 0.4873 and the OWIF score is 1. Thus, the total score of all the five evaluative techniques is 184.9 and the average is 37. The Composite Rank is 20 and the Institutional Rank is 17.

5

Implications of Library Website Assessment

5.1. INTRODUCTION

Library websites have been instrumental in changing both the means of communicating with users and the nature and range of service provided along with the entire set of professional tools used by the librarians. It is a digital gate to library services and resources (Salisbury & Griffis, 2014). Library websites are being used in abundance by different kinds of users specifically within and outside the campus (Arsha & Ameen, 2015). A well-updated library website should provide online information about traditional library collections and services, access provision to online resources, perform information services online, guide and educate users, communicate space management for library users (feedback and lodging complaints), promote the library and its website (Mierzecka & Suminas, 2016). Library websites should communicate library mission statements and allow better understanding for stakeholders (Kuchi, 2006). The library website is the primary source of information for users. The important part of any website is that it should be regularly up dated and information should be easily accessible (Verma & Devi, 2016). Various institutions have developed library websites that provide information regarding various facilities, resources and services offered to their users and to fulfill their information requirements.

5.2. OBSERVATIONS

5.2.1. Web Indicators Observations

The five blocks were examined meticulously to ascertain the percentage availability of web indicators in specific institutional libraries. The web indicators, their presence or absence, has been discussed block wise.

I. Resource Block

An institutional library exists to support the parent organization. Its proper usage helps students, researchers and others to overcome the barriers and other discouragements to information access. It helps users to achieve their academic pursuits. Library website serves as source for enhancing the quality of education of the library users. The performance of the institutional libraries on specific web indicators shows that:

1. E-database : If list of E-Data Base is mentioned on a website it would be user friendly because of ease of operation. Users can fruitfully enhance this search.There were 12 per cent of the library websites that did not mention the e-databases on their library websites. These libraries were IARI, IITH and IIITH. The remaining 88 per cent of the library websites had included this feature. Thus, 12 per cent of the library websites were not providing user friendly search features which could enhance their functioning.

2. Tutorials on Library Related Topics : The observations showed that 96% of the institutional library websites did not mention tutorials on library related topics. Only one library website, namely, IIT Roorkee, had mentioned the availability of this indicator.Tutorials on library related topics are mentioned on library websites and can be helpful to users. These tutorials are designed to teach the user how to use the library in a proper way. As this feature was absent in 96 percent of the library websites it shows that they were rather impoverished and should feature in this essential facility.

3. Dictionaries and Encyclopedias : There were 60 per cent of the institutional library websites that did not have this feature. The websites were namely IITK, IITB, IITD, IISERP, IITBBS, THU, IITM, IMSC, NITT, NITC, NITK, IARI, TIRF, JNCARS and IISERK. These are reference collections of the library. The details are mentioned on library website and serve as a backbone to the library. It was observed that 60 per cent of these library websites did not have this feature which is a very significant observation. The above websites should incorporate this feature definitely.

4. Subject Bibliographies : There were 48 per cent of the institutional library websites that did not have the feature of Subject Bibliographics. The ones that did not have this feature were namely IITB, NITR, IITBBS, IITM, NITC, NITK, JNCARS, IITH, TIRF, SINP, NITT and IARI. These are books or pamphlets with bibliographic listings of works on a single subject. Their availability on the library website is very useful for research scholars and faculty alike. The fact that 48 per cent of the library websites do not that have this feature shows its deficiency.

5. Referencing Tool : There were 48 per cent of the library websites that did not have the referencing tool. They were representing the following institutions namely, IISERP, IITBBS, THU, BITP, SINP, NITT, NITC, NITK, IARI, JNCARS, IIITH and IISERK. Referencing tools help to know about the citation style required by the users. The 48 per cent library websites that did not have this tool should definitely install it.

6. Course Materials : On the availability of course materials on the library websites it was observed that 56 per cent of the institutional library websites did not carry the requisite course materials. The library websites that did not display the course materials were, namely, IISERP, THU, BITP, IITM, ISBH, IMSC, SINP, NITT, NITC, IARI, IITH, IIITH, IISERK and TIRF. Mentioning of required course materials on the library websites is essential to add to the user's ease of the students.

7. Reading List Recommended by the Faculty : There were 76 per cent of the institutional library websites that did not display a reading list recommended by the faculty. These were: IIMA, IISERP, IITBBS, IITB, THU, BITP, IITKG, ISBH, SINP, NITT, NITC, NITK, JNCARS, IITH, IIITH, IISERK, IMSC, IARI and TIRF. There were 24 per cent of the library websites that carried the reading list recommended by the faculty. This list can help avoid any duplicity as the list is constantly mentioned on the library website.

8. Library Glossary : There were 100 per cent of the institutional library websites that did not have a library glossary whereas it is a brief description of the terminology commonly used in the library. This is a helpful tool for the new users.

9. Publications of Academic Staff : There were 76 per cent of the institutional library websites that did not display the publications of the academic staff. These websites were namely: NITR, IITBBS, IITR, IITB, THU, BITP, IITKG, IITM, ISBH, IMSC, SINP, NITT, NITC, NITK, JNCARS, IITH, IIITH, IISERK and TIRF. The publications of the academic staff are essentially available on the library websites and can enhance scholarly communication. The above websites should most definitively be worked upon to add in this feature.

10. Past Year Question Paper : A list of the past year's questions is posted on the institutional library website to help students study the pattern of appearance of the question paper. There were 96 per cent of the institutional library websites that were not displaying the past years' question papers. These websites were: NITR, IIMA, IITD, IITK, IITR, IITB, IITG, IISERP, IITBBS, THU, BITP, IITM, ISBH, IMSC, SINP, NITT, NITC, NITK, IARI, JNCARS, IITH, IIITH, IISERK and TIRF. They should put up these past years questions to facilitate the users.

11. Newspaper Clipping : There were 80 per cent of the library websites that did not carry newspaper clippings. The names of these institutions are IIMA, IITD, IITG, IITKG, IITM, IITK, IISERP, IITBBS, IITB, ISBH, IMSC, NITT, NITC, NITK, IARI, JNCARS, IITH, IIITH, IISERK and TIRF. Exploring clippings of newspapers on the library websites related to various institutions can help libraries in reaching out to users wherever they are and enables them to save time. The newspaper clippings are also called press clippings. The library website of Jawaharlal Nehru University, Delhi is the best example of newspaper clippings. It was interesting to note that 80 per cent did not have this vital facility.

12. New Arrivals : There were 64 per cent of the institutional library websites that gave adequate coverage to new arrivals. These websites were: IISERP, THU, IITD, BITP, IITKG, IITM, IMSC, SINP, NITT, IITH, IITG, ISBH, NITC, TIRF, IIITH and IISERK. Notification and exhibition of new arrivals on library websites enhances user's satisfaction and credibility of the library as users need awareness on upcoming list of books.

13. Online Reference Chat : Online Reference Chat provides library services beyond library hours. It offers a support system for the users information needs. Online Reference Chat is an innovative and cost effective service provided by the library. It is a live chat that is available and accessible 24 by 7 from anywhere. All 25 of the institutional library websites declined giving the users access to Online Reference Chat facility.

14. Library Podcast : Library Podcast serves as an array of learning materials that users require. It can be a good experience for the librarian as well as users. Podcast includes both audio and video medium. Any sort of library information can be served as Library Podcast for example, the virtual book club, etc. There were 92 per cent of the institutional library websites that did not have this feature of Library Podcast available to their active library website users. These were: IITB, IIMA, IITD, IITK, IITR, IITG, IISERP, IITBBS, BITP, IITKG, IITM, ISBH, IMSC, SINP, NITT, NITC, NITK, IARI, JNCARS, IITH, IIITH, IISERK and TIRF. This is an essential service that should be available on all library websites.

II. Service Block

The web indicators within this block show the status of the institutional library websites. The web indicators have been dealt with exclusively.

1. OPAC : There were 16 per cent of the institutional library websites that did not have this service available on their websites. These were IITH, IITR, IIITH and IISERK. OPAC is an online public access catalogue. Users search a library catalogue primarily to find books and other material available in a library. OPAC is a gateway to library collection and is now-a-days essential for all libraries. It is therefore necessary that all library websites make this an essential feature.

2. Inter Library Loans (ILL) : Inter Library Loan is a service whereby a patron of one library can borrow books DVDs, etc. that are owned by another library. ILL allows the broadening of the scope of research by facilitating the use of materials which are not owned by the library. There were 28 per cent of the institutional library websites that did not have the facility of providing access to Inter Library Loans. These institutions were IITG, SINP, IITK, NITC,

IITH, IIITH and IISERK. These institutions should rapidly feature in this service.

3. Online Feedbacks : Among all the websites there were 84 per cent that could not provide the facility of Online Feedback to their users. These institutions were IITB, IITR, NITR, IIMA, IITD, IITG, IISERP, IITBBS, THU, BITP, IITKG, ISBH, IMSC, NITT, NITC, NITK, JNCARS, IITH, IIITH, IISERK and TIRF. Online feedback can be an extremely useful means of efficiently gathering data about the library users attributes, knowledge, behavior, experience, demographics, satisfaction level etc. After getting the feedback the libraries can enhance their future planning. It is significant to note that 84 per cent of the library websites do not have this essential service.

4. Online Book Reservation : This service was not available to 40 per cent of the institutional library websites. These were namely, SINP, NITT, NITC, IITG, IITM, IARI, JNCARS, IITH, IIITH and IISERK. Libraries are becoming interactive now-a-days. A variety of users desire to use them. Librarians can approve or reject the online request according to the availability of books in the library. In this fast paced age it is essential that this service be available to all library websites.

5. E-Mail Reference of Librarian : The supplying of references through email is a library service intended for distance users. The information on this service helps users submit any query any time to the librarian and the librarian can answer according to the specific email reference library policy. There were only 16 percent of the institutional library websites that did not have this information. These institutions were, namely, IARI, IISERP, IISERK and TIRF.

6. Virtual Users Training Sessions : Now–a-days libraries provide virtual training to users to enrich them. For example - INFLIBNET Centre suggests and advocates for Virtual Library of India. There were 88 per cent of the institutional library websites that could not provide this service to the users. The names of these institutions are: IITD, IITG, IISERP, IITBBS, IITK, NITR, IIMA, ISBH, IMSC, SINP, NITT, NITC, THU, BITP, IITM, NITK, IARI, JNCARS, IITH, IIITH, IISERK and TRIF. They should all have this facility.

7. Online Orientation Session : Overall 80 per cent of the institutional websites were not providing these services. The names of these institutions are: IIMA, IITD, IITG, IITK, NITR, IITBBS, THU, BITP, IITKG, ISBH, IMSC, SINP, NITT, NITC, NITK, IARI, JNCARS, IITH, IIITH and TIRF. Orientation pertaining to the library for new users through online explaining to them about the comprehensive resources and dynamic services offered by the library to support research, teaching and learning needs. New users and new students can learn about the resources and services even before their classes begin. This is a very useful library input and should be used extensively among all libraries.

8. Document Delivery Service (DDS) : DDS is provided free or at normal cost. Delivery time is 7-10 days either in electronic or print version. For this the user has to submit a requisite DDS request. Information of this service on the library websites is most helpful for remote users. There were 48 per cent of the institutional library websites that did not offer document delivery services to the website users. These institutions were: IITD, IITG, BITP, IARI, IITH, IIITH, IISERK, TIRF, IITM, SINP, NITT and NITC. These 48 per cent library websites need to enhance this aspect of their service.

9. Digital Communication Forum : All the websites were not providing the Digital Communication Forum services to their users. Thus, this service was not available in any of the 25 institutional library websites studied. To reinforce scholarly communication the DCF is crucial for libraries now-a-days. It strengthens and transforms learning to a higher level. Its information and usage enhances the institutional research and learning. Therefore, all libraries should add it to their repertoire.

III. Links Block

The following is a presentation of the links provided by the various websites of Libraries in 25 institutions.

1. Links to Course and Study Program Sites : There were 60 per cent of the institutional library websites that did not have this facility. Their names are BITP, ISBH, IMSC, NITT, IITG, IISERP, THU, NITC NITK, IARI, JNCARS, IITH, IIITH, IISERK and TIRF. Now-a-days, providing information about Courses and Study Programs on library websites are the need of the hour for example MOOCs (Massive Open Online Courses) are offered for free to anyone interested in taking them. This large gap needs to be addressed immediately.

2. Links to Parent Institutions : Link to parent institutions is necessary as sometimes users tend to get disoriented while going deep into the website or they have to begin a new task if they are on a wrong page. There were only 8 per cent of the institutional library websites where the link to the Parent Institutions was not available. These were namely, JNCARS and TIRF. Therefore, it is favorable that most of the library websites have this link.

3. Link to Information Manuals : Among all the websites there were 84 per cent that did not provide their users with links to Information Manuals. These institutions are listed as: IITK, IITR, IIMA, IITG, IISERP, IITBBS, THU, IITKG, IITM, ISBH, IMSC, SINP NITT, NITC, NITK, IARI, JNCARS, IITH, IIITH, IISERK and TIRF. Information Manuals offer additional details and greater insights on key topics of relevance. The details given on the website should be helpful for users of the library. This glaring fact cannot be ignored. This essential feature was missing in 84 per cent of the library websites.

4. Free Internet Resources : There were only 4 per cent of the websites that did not have access to free internet resources. This institution was ITG. There are several free resources available on the net for users. For example Reading Apps on various subjects, etc.

5. Links to Download Necessary Software : There were 60 per cent of the institutional library websites that do not offer links to download necessary software. These institutions are IISERP, THU, BITP, IITM, NITK, IARI, ISBH, IMSC, IIITH, IISERK, NITT, NITC, TIRF, JNCARS and IITH. If links to download necessary software are available on library websites it enables more users to like them and to use them. It is also necessary to upgrade this software from time to time on the library website. It would be a good idea if all libraries' websites could have this facility.

6. Link to Search Engines : Links to Search Engines on library websites save the time of the user. Without Search Engines, users would have to look at sites one by one and pore over the contents of each carefully which can prove to be a tedious prospect. There were 88 per cent of the library websites that did not provide any links to search engines. These were IITB, IITD, IISERP, IITBBS, THU, BITP, IITKG, ISBH, IMSC, NITT, NITC, NITK, IARI, JNCARS, IIMA, NITR, IITM, SINP, IIITH, IISERK and TIRF.

7. Links to Related Libraries : There were 68 percent of the libraries that did not have Links to Related Libraries. These institutions were: TIRF, IITB, IITD, IISERP, IITBBS, THU, BITP, IITKG, ISBH, IMSC, NITT, NITC, NITK, IARI, JNCARS, IIITH and IISERK. Information Provided on Library Websites regarding Links to related libraries leads to resource efficiency through sharing resources. It is advisable that these 68 per cent libraries work to add in this feature on their websites.

8. Links to OPAC of other Libraries : There were only 16 per cent of these institutional library websites that did not have the potential to provide links to OPAC of other libraries. These were namely, IITH, IIITH, IISERK and TIRF. Web OPAC services are a gateway to the resources of other libraries as it is and therefore all library websites should use them.

IV. Information Block

1. Mission Statement : There were 76 per cent of the institutions that did not have the Mission Statement on the institutional library website. The names of these institutions are: IITR, IITB, IIMA, IITD, IITG, THU, BITP, IITKG, IITM, ISBH, IMSC, SINP, NITC, NITK, IARI, JNCARS, IIITH, IISERK and TIRF. The library should work with the vision set by the library management to complete its mission i.e. user satisfaction. These statements are important to design strategy for the library. This information on library websites works as a mirror image of the library in itself. Therefore it is advisable that the library websites incorporate a Mission Statement and work upon it.

2. Floor Plan : There were 68 per cent of the institutional library websites that did not give the Floor Plan of the institution. These institutions were: IITR, IIMA, IITG, IITBBS, THU, IITKG, ISBH, SINP, NITT, NITC, NITK, IARI, JNCARS, IITH, IIITH, IISERK and TIRF. These library websites most definitively should incorporate this aspect to facilitate their users. If the detailed Floor Plan and Lay Out of the library is mentioned on the library website it helps new users to search for what is available at whichever place in the library in an easy manner.

3. Site Map : The sitemap protocol allows a webmaster to inform search engines about URL's on a website that are available for cruising library Site Maps. There were 92 per cent of the library websites that did not provide the Site Map of the institutions on the website. These institutions were: IITK, IITR, IITB, NITR, IIMA, IITD, IISERP, IITBBS, THU, IITKG, IITM, ISBH, IMSC, SINP, NITT, NITC, NITK, IARI, JNCARS, IITH, IIITH, TIRF and IISERK.

4. Web Master Contact Details : There were 96 percent of the library websites that did not give the Contact Details of the Web Master on the website. These institutes were, namely, IITK, IITR, IITB, NITR, IIMA, IITD, IITG, IISERP, IITBBS, THU, BITS, IITKG, IITM, ISBH, IMSC, SINP, NITT, NITC, NITK, IARI, IITH, IIITH, TIRF and IISERK. If details of web masters are available on library websites then the user can contact the relevant webmaster if he faces any problem while using the website. Interestingly, this does not seem to be a very great priority with the institutional library websites.

5. Staff Members Biography : Details of the staff of the library are necessary on library websites. It saves the time of the users. Users can directly contact the required staff members for a particular staff biography. These were 24 per cent of the library websites that did not give the Staff Members Biography on the institutional library website. These institutions were namely IISERP, ISBH, IARI, IISERK, SINP and TIRF. Most libraries were having this provision on their websites which seems quite an attainment.

6. Photographs of Staff Members : There were 56 per cent of the library websites that did not carry the Photographs of Staff Members. These institutions are, namely, IITK, IISERP, IITBBS, THU, BITP, IITM, ISBH, IMSC, SINP, NITT, IARI, JNCARS, TIRF and IISERK. It helps in the recognition of the staff of the library and therefore is essential for the users.

7. Visitor Number : It helps to know exactly how many users visited the library website. Higher the number of users, higher will be the creditability of the website and vice versa. There were 84 per cent of the library websites that did not display the Visitor Number. These were IITR, IITB, IIMA, IITG, IISERP, IITBBS, THU, BITP, IITKG, IITM, ISBH, IMSC, NITT, NITC, NITK, IARI, JNCARS, IITH, IIITH, IISERK and TIRF. These library websites cannot provide useful feedback to users. This facility should be essentially available on the library website to the user.

8. Help Guide : There were 44 per cent of the institutional library websites that did not have a Help Guide for the users. These institutions were, IITG, BITP, ISBH, NITT, NITC, IARI, JNCARS, IITH, IIITH, IISERK and TIRF. Information of the Help Guide helps users understand how to make the best use of the library. Absence of this facility discourages and deters potential users.

9. Contact Information : It was observed that the requisite Contact Information was not available in 16 per cent of the library websites. These institutes were IITH, IIITH, IISERK and TIRF. As the contact information of the library helps the users in getting in touch with the library it is essential that this facility be upgraded in the library websites that are lacking it.

10. Opening Hours : The library websites that did not have information about the Opening Hours of the library belonged to the following 24 per cent, namely, SINP, IARI, IITH, IIITH, IISERK and TIRF. Opening Hours is necessary information of the library which all users must have. By knowing the 'Opening hours' a user can plan his or her visit to the library. Therefore, it is necessary that this information be present in all library websites.

11. Staff Directory : There were 20 per cent library websites that did not adequately display the Staff Directory of the library. These library websites belonged to the following institutions – ISBH, SINP, IARI, IISERK and TIRF. The Staff Directory helps the user to know the staff of the library. Most of the library websites ensured that this information was available for the user.

12. Copyright Statement : Among the library websites examined there were 36 per cent that did not have the Copyright Statement. These institutions were IITK, IITB, NITR, IITKG, IITM, ISBH, JNCARS, IISERK and

TIRF. Putting the copyright notice at the bottom of a site states that the material displayed is not to be used without permission of the owner. It is an essential part of the website development that ensures originality of the material and making sure the material will not be copied.

13. Holiday Calendar : There were 80 per cent of the library websites that did not display the Holiday Calendar of the respective institutions. These websites were of the following institutions IITB, IITK, IITD, IISERP, IITBBS, THU, BITP, IITKG, IITM, IMSC SINP, NITT, NITC, NITK, IARI, JNCARS, IITH, IIITH, IISERK and TRIF. Information regarding the library's Holiday Calendar on the library website helps the users manage their time fruitfully. But it does not seem to be a popular facility on the institutional library websites nor does it seem to be a priority with them.

14. Rules and Regulations : Only 24 per cent of the total institutional library websites did not display the Rules and Regulations on the website pages. These institutions were – NITC, IARI, IITH, IIITH, IISERK and TRIF. These are general instructions on how to use a library for creating a better environment. It helps to keep the user in check of all aspects so that the institution can move ahead efficiently and effectively.

15. Online and In-House Facilities : In-house refers to the conducting of an activity or operation within a library whereas online facilities are the web based library services. For example e-reference service, Web Based Resources etc. The information about these facilities is on the net. Among the 24 per cent websites that did not display the Online and In-house Facilities were the library websites like ISBH, NITK, JNCARS, IITH, IIITH and IISERK.

16. Library News : There were 36 per cent of the institutional library websites that did not carry the Library News at all. These institutions were IISERP, IITM, NITT, IARI, JNCARS, IITH, IIITH, IISERK and TRIF. Library news helps users to provide information about whatever events are happening in the library during that particular time. Therefore, it is necessary to have this feature on the library website as an essentiality.

17. Library History : Among the institutional library websites there were 36 per cent that did not post the Library History on the website. These belonged to institutions namely THU, NITT, NITC, IARI, IMSC, IIITH, IITH, IISERK and TRIF. It helps users obtain information about when the library was formed. The type and size of collection it has? What are the major strengths of the library? This is a useful facility for the library website.

18. FAQ's : FAQ's are frequently asked questions and their answers. These are questions supposedly asked commonly about the library content on the library websites. The format is generally used on e-mailing lists and other online platforms. This is a vital service that should be on every library website. It is deplorable that 68 per cent did not have this service at the time of the research investigation. These library websites belonged to IITR, IITD, IISERP, THU, BITP, IITKG, IITM, IMSC, SINP, NITT, NITC, IARI, JNCARS and IITH.

19. Institutions Full Name : There were only one (4 per cent) institutional library website that did not display the Institution's Full Name i.e. JNCARS. The information about the Institutional Full Name on the library website would help to increase the spectrum of library. This was available on all library websites barring one.

20. Library Policies : Library Policies are carefully designed, broadly stated, written guidelines for actions and decisions of a library. It is the governing principle formally adopted by the Library Committee. The Library Polices were not displayed on the 60 per cent of institutional library websites. These institutional library websites are, IITR, NITR, IITG, IITBBS, THU, BITP, SINP, NITT, NITC, NITK, IARI, IITH, IIITH, IISERK and TRIF.

These institutions should rapidly incorporate this feature as it is most essential for all library website users.

V. Design & Graphic Block

1. Memorable URL : If the URL of the library website is memorable it will be easy to track the website.There were only 4 per cent of the institutional library websites that did not display the memorable URL. The NITT library website did not have this feature.

2. Website is Consistent in Layout : If the library website is consistent in layout it shows the overall outlook of the library website. Layout refers to basic framework and structure of the library website. All the Institutional Library Websites have a Consistent Layout.

3. Hyperlink Identity : There were 48 per cent of the library websites that did not have a Hyperlink Identity. The institutions that did not carried these characteristics are IITK, IITM, ISBH, IITD, SINP, BITP, IITKG, NITT, NITC, IARI, IIITH and TIRF. The hyperlink is a reference to data that users can directly follow by clicking on it. It points to a specific element within a document. The institutional library websites that do not have this feature should incorporate it with immediate effect.

4. Homepage Length is in One Screenful : There were 88 per cent of the library websites that did not have the Homepage Length in One Screenful. This was true of the following institutions IITK, IITR, IITB, NITR, IIMA, IITD, IITG, IISERP, IITBBS, THU, BITP, IITKG, ISBH, IMSC, SINP, NITT, NITK, IARI, IITH, IIITH, IISERK and TIRF. If the homepage length is in one screenful it will be the easiest way for users to visualize it. This is a facilitative feature and should be on the library website to promote ease of usage by users.

5. Date of Last Website Update : There were 80 per cent of the institutional library websites that did not display the Date of Last Website Update. This was true of the following institutions, IIMA, IITK, IITR, IITB, NITR, IITBBS, THU, BITP, IITKG, ISBH, IMSC, SINP, NITT, NITC, NITK, IARI, JNCARS, IIITH, IISERK and TIRF. It is important for users to know about when the library website was last refreshed. Old websites have more broken links and fossil information. Thus, this information is necessary for all library website studied here.

6. Avoid Flash Animation : There were 36 per cent of the institutions that did not Avoid Flash Animation on their library websites. These institutions were IITK, IITR, IITD, IITBBS, IITKG, SINP, NITC, NITK and IIITH. If there are more flash animations it leads to the slowing down of the library website load time. Thus, the user gets irritated and looses interest in the website.

7. Avoid Background Sounds : All the library websites Avoid Background Sounds. These sounds may be irritating to the ears and the main focus of the users tends to get disturbed.

8. Avoid Horizontal Scrolling : All the library websites Avoid Horizontal Scrolling. By default the scrolling in the website should be vertical instead of horizontal as vertical scrolling helps user to search the website systematically and in a better way. It was an appreciable fact that all of the institutional library websites had this feature.

9. Has Access to Home Page from all other Pages: This is the best practice of the website that there should be access to Home Page from all other pages of the website. As homepage serves as a new starting point for those who are on the wrong page of the website. There were no library websites that did not have Access to the Home Page from all other pages. Thus, all library websites had this facility.

10. Accessible through Chrome and Firefox : Search Engines make the internet work by making its billons of webpages searchable. No search engine is perfect; however, the internet is vast and growing every moment. Therefore, it makes sense that the website should be accessible through different Search Engines. This was applicable to all the library websites.

11. Providing Text Only Option : If the internet connection is slow then loading pages with many images can prove to be a hassle. Therefore, the text option is considered much better with a few images. All the institutional library websites support the 'Provide Text Only Option'.

12. Use of Descriptive Headings : Descriptive Headings and titles work together to give users an overview of the content of the library. Descriptive headings identify sections of content in relation to the webpage as a whole and to other sections of the same webpage. All institutional Library Websites had exhibited the use of Descriptive Headings. There were no institutions that did not have this feature.

13. Use of Heading's Tag Consistently : Heading Tags are tags that are used for creation of headings. These tags should be consistent as the Search Engines generally give priority to the Headings as a keyword of a website. There were only 20 per cent of the institutional library websites that did not have this feature. The names of the institutions were IITD, IISERP, NITC, NITK and JNCARS. They should adopt this feature as it facilitates the search of the users.

14. Functional through Keyboard : Websites should be functional both through mouse and keyboard as it saves the time of the user and satisfied his or her searching on the website. All the institutional library websites were functional through Keyboard.

15. Multilingual : The website should adopt multilingual software to enhance the number of users. For example, most of the Indian Government Websites are found to be bilingual that is the text is in Hindi and English. There were 84 per cent of the institutional library websites that were not multilingual. These were namely, IITK, IITR, IITB, NITR, THU, BITP, IITKG, IIMA, IITM, ISBH, IMSC, SINP, NITC, NITK, JNCARS, IIITH, IISERK, TIRF, IITD, IITG and IITBBS. This is a very useful feature and should be an essential part of all library websites to facilitate the domestic and international users.

16. Do not Blink : Websites should not blink as this tends to lose the interest of the user because users generally judge the value of a website in a matter of seconds. There were 64 per cent of the institutions studied that did not have the Do Not Blink feature. These institutions were: IITK, IITR, IITB, NITR, IIMA, IITD, IITG, IISERP, IITBBS, BITP, IITKG, SINP, NITC, NITK, IITH and IIITH. To maintain the interest of the users the library websites should ensure that this feature is incorporated.

17. Write Abbreviations in the First Instance : If using abbreviations, it is advisable to provide the full form before proving the abbreviated form. There were 88 per cent of the institutional library websites that did not have the provision to write abbreviation in the first instance. These institutions are IITK, IITR, IITB, NITR, IIMA, IITD, IITG, IITBBS, BITP, IITKG, IITM, ISBH, IMSC, SINP, NITT, NITK, IARI, JNCARS, IITH, IIITH, IISERK and TIRF.

18. Don't Use Underline Unless it is Hyperlink : If links are underlined they are easy to find because users understand that underlined text means that it is a link. The underlined form draws their attention and therefore should be used. There were 16 per cent of the institutional library websites that did not use this feature. Their names are IITB, IITM, IMSC, NITK.

19. Use High Contrast of Text : If the text is of a contrasting color to the background it is easy to read. The best example is white background with black text. Among the 25 institutions observed there were 32 per cent that did not avail themselves of the option of use high contrast of text. These Institutions were NITT, IITH, NITC, NITK,

IIITH, IISERK, JNCARS and TIRF. These library websites should improve their legibility by improving their color contrast.

20. Avoid Long Text Blocks : There were 84 percent of the library websites that did not adhere to the basic premise for websites to avoid long text blocks. These institutions were IITK, IITR, NITR, IIMA, IITD, IITG, IISERP, IITBBS, THU, BITP, IITKG, ISBH, IMSC, SINP, NITT, NITK, JNCARS, IITH, IIITH, IISERK, TRIF, JNCARS, IITH, IIITH, IISERK and TIRF. The webmaster should avoid long text blocks with illustrations, as the potential user is not impressed by large amounts of text. Rather they tend to get intimidated by it. These library websites should follow this feature as a guideline.

21. Headlines that Support Meta Tag : Meta Tags are snippets of text that describe a page's content. The meta tags do not appear on the page itself but only in the pages code. Thus, Headings should support Meta tags as they are little content descriptions that help search engines what a web page is about. All the websites support this feature.

22. Use Left Justify : There were only 8 per cent of the institutional library websites that did not use left justify. These institutions were NITK and IITH. If the website is in left justify it will be easier for users to read the text of the website.

23. Strong Visual Identity : The website should support bright saturated colors. The font should be appropriate so that the visual identity of the website looks strong. There were 24 per cent of the library websites that did not show strong visual identity. These websites belonged to the following institutions, namely, IMSC, JNCARS, NITC, NITK, IITH and TIRF. These websites should strengthen their visual identity.

24. Use Visual Consistency Across All Pages : There are 20 per cent of the library websites that did not use visual consistency across all pages. The institutions were NITC, NITK, IITH, TIRF and JNCARS. There should be even, visual consistency across all the pages of the website. The above websites should adhere to this necessity.

25. Include Links to Return to Homepage : There were only 8 per cent of the library websites that did not include links to return to homepage. These institutions were IARI and TIRF. All pages of a website should return to homepage. These two websites should ensure this feature to increase the reliability of their users.

26. Well Designed Error Screen : A well designed error screen or complaint box at the bottom of the website is necessary because it helps to improve the website if feedback can be obtained from users and guide the webmasters in the right direction. There were 68 per cent of the institutional library websites that did not have a well designed error screen. These institutions were: IITK, IITR, NITR, IIMA, IITD, IITG, IISERP, IITBBS, IITKG, IITM, SINP, NITT, NITC, NITK, JNCARS, IIITH and TIRF. It is essential that all these library websites should be upgraded so that they have well designed error screen.

27. Consistence in Navigation Elements : If the navigation elements are consistent then users feel comfortable when they cite a website. The user should get the feel that the website is designed, arranged and has logical information. If the navigation is consistent in a website it can satisfy the users and compel them to return to the same website. Consistency can be maintained by correct use of tabs, good use of fonts and layout, that is the basic framework and structure of the website. There were 24 per cent of the institutional library websites studied that do not have consistence in navigation elements. These institutions are NITR, IITM, JNCARS, IITH, IIITH and TIRF. To facilitate ease of usage these websites should be upgraded and equipped with this essential feature.

28. Internal Search Engine : An Internal Search Engine allows searching within a site for pages containing certain keywords. The Internal Search Engine is particularly useful on large sites as an alternative to hierarchical menus for site navigation. It is essential for a library website so that the search can be easily sorted and save the time of the user.There were 28 per cent of the institutional library websites that did not have Internal Search Engines in place. The institutions were IITG, IITKG, IITM, NITT, NITK, IARI and JNCARS. These sites must have in place an internet search engine as it is necessary to save user time.

29. Short Menus : Short Menus are the rows or strip of menu items' titles that when clicked displayed the dropdown menu of other items or commands. A short menu bar is an integral Graphical User Interface (GUI) component for a variety of software application windows. These menus make it easier for the user to browse. These menu bars are always visible and available on the website. Among the 25 institutions studied there were a significant 56 per cent that did not have short menus. The Institutional library websites that did not have these were IITK, IITB, NITR, IITD, IITG, IISERP, IITBBS, IITKG, IITM, IMSC, SINP, NITK, JNCARS and IITH. These websites should work on getting short menus.

30. Multiple Access Facilities : There were 12 per cent of the library websites studied that did not have Multiple Access Facilities. These belonged to the following institutions namely IITM, IMSC and JNCARS. Multiple access allows several terminals connected to the transmission medium to transmit over it. It improves the overall capacity over a geographical area by permitting the available bandwidth to be used simultaneously by different users. The multiple access method permits networking across various terminals to connect to the same multipoint transmission medium to transmit over it and share its capacity. For example, the Wireless

Network, Ring Network, Star Networks, etc.

31. Use of Navigational Aids : Navigational aids provide direct assistance with site navigation. It is used while designing the website. Without such navigation aids the website can appear unstructured and disorganized. Tools are a clear indication that the website content is of knowledge and depth. Among the institutions studied almost all that is 92 per cent of their library websites did not use navigational aids. These institutions were namely, IITK, IITR, NITR, IIMA, IITD, IISERP, IITBBS, THU, BITP, IITKG, IITM, ISBH, IMSC, SINP, NITT, NITC, NITK, IARI, JNCARS, IITH, IIITH, IISERK and TIRF.

32. Relative Font Size : There were only 20 per cent of the institutional library websites studied that did not have a relative font size. These institutions were namely NITR, IITM, JNCARS, IITH and IIITH. The website should have explicit visibility for the user. The text should be clear throughout the entire page of the website in a relatively visible font size.

33. Headings for Tables : Headings for Tables help display the data and layout of a website. The table caption tag helps summarize the content displayed under it. The Table heading tag <th> is used to identify cells that are either row or column headers.There were only 4 per cent of the institutional library websites that did not have any Headings for Tables. The institution library website that did not have this feature was IITM.

34. Large Graphics : There were 72 per cent of the institutions that did not have large graphics on their library websites. These institutions were IITK, NITR, IITD, IITG, ISERP, IITBBS, THU, IITM, ISBH, IMSC, SNIP, NITK, IARI, JNCARS, IITH, IIITH, IISERK and TIRF. The large graphics make impressive visual impact on a website. These graphics should fit in with the purpose, organization and style of the page. They also help to focus the ideas or the contents of the website. Therefore, all websites should have this feature.

35. Avoid Non-Standard HTML Codes : Non standard HTML codes can affect the search engine. All the library websites almost tried to avoid non-standard HTML codes.

36. Headlines that Support Scanning : Good website design promotes efficient scanning. It is helpful for scanning web pages quickly. Headings are used to group similar content and to highlight important items and sections within a page. All the library websites support scanning.

37. Do not Present Information through Colours: Colours that are too bright to read can cause problems when paired with dark backgrounds. There were only 12 per cent of the institutional library websites that did not have this feature. The names of these institutions were IITKG, IITM, IITH, IIITH and IISERK.

38. Avoid Use of title like "Click Here" : The term 'click' is irrelevant to many assistive technologies and is not descriptive enough for users. Using the world "click" on links takes the user's attention away from the interface and on to their mouse. Seventy six percent of institutional library websites i.e., IITK, IITR, IITB, NITR, IIMA, IITD, IITG, IISERP, IITBBS, THU, BITP, IMSC, SINP, NITT, NITC, NITK, IARI, JNCARS, TIRF found avoiding use of titles like click here whereas twenty four percent of institutional library websites i.e., IITKG, IITM, ISBH, IITH, IIITH, IISERK are using such titles.

39. Use Hotspot : Hotspot (Wi-Fi) is a physical location where people may obtain internet access, typically using Wi-Fi technology.There were 68 per cent of the library websites that do not use Hotspot. These institutions were IITK, IITB, IITD, IISERP, THU, BITP, IITKG, ISBH, IMSC, NITT, NITK, IARI, JNCARS, IITH, IIITH, IISERK and TIRF. This is an essentiality that must be incorporated into the library website.

40. Print Friendly : If the website is print friendly

then the user can download the PDF and take prints. Print friendly design essentially removes unnecessary web elements and focuses on content alone. Almost 96 per cent, of the library websites were not print friendly. The names of these institutions are: IITK, IITB, NITR, IIMA, IITD, IITG, IISERP, IITBBS, THU, BITP, IITKG, IITM, ISBH, IMSC, SINP, NITT, NITC, NITK, IARI, JNCARS, IITH, IIITH, IISERK and TIRF. It is regrettable that these library websites are not print friendly.

41. Avoid Italics For Large Text : The use of Italics on the web can have a bad impact on the accessibility of the website as the Italics font is difficult to read. There were just 12 per cent of the library websites of the 25 institutions being studied that did not adhere to avoid Italics for large text. These institutions were NITR, IITBBS and TIRF. They should incorporate this feature in their library websites.

42. Line Length Within 10-12 Words per Line : This rule was not followed by 88 per cent of the institutional library websites. The institutions names are: IITR, IITB, NITR, IIMA, IITD, IITG, IISERP, IITBBS, THU, BITP, IITKG, ISBH, IMSC, SINP, NITT, NITK, IARI, JNCARS, IITH, IIITH, IISERK and TIRF. For optimum reading and legibility of website, it is important to have 10-12 words per line or 50-60 characters per line only. If this is not followed then the user will finding the website text to be tedious and will lose interest very shortly. The above library websites would be well advised to adhere to this clause for the benefit of the users.

43. Font Type 'Georgia' for Web Pages : Among the library websites studied 76 per cent were not using font type 'Georgia' for web pages. The names of these institutions are: IITK, IITR, IITB, IISERP, IITBBS, THU, BITP, IITKG, IITM, ISBH, IMSC, SINP, NITT, NITC, NITK, IARI, JNCARS, IITH and IISERK. The 'Georgia' font type is the perfect font for web design. It gives a favorable impact of the website and shows a massive improvement in the layout. This makes the website more legible. The 'Georgia' font is also known as a standard, web-safe font for the website. However, 76 percent of the websites have not used 'Georgia' font. They will probably realize its usefulness and change over to in soon.

44. Use Graphics Sparingly : Graphics should be used sparingly to maintain quality. It is generally a feature used to attract the user's attention, communicate effectively with the reading audience. It signifies what the website stands for and effectively presents the company's profile. This indicator was absent in 84 per cent of the institutional library websites. The names of the institutions that did not adhere to this principle are namely, IITR, NITR, IIMA, IITD, IITG, IISERP, IITBBS, THU, BITP, IITKG, IITM, ISBH, SINP, NITT, NITC, NITK, IARI, JNCARS, IIITH, IISERK and TIRF. These websites need to cut down on the use of large graphics.

45. Font Type "Times New Roman" for Heavy Text: There were 80 per cent of the library websites that did not use font type "Times New Roman" for heavy text. The institutes hosting these library websites were IITR, IITB, IIMA, IITG, IISERP, IITBBS, THU, BITP, IITKG, IITM, ISBH, IMSC, SINP, NITC, NITK, IARI, JNCARS, IIITH, IISERK and TIRF. The Times New Roman font is a good font to use for text in heavy documents and provides huge impact to the website. Thus, it is advisable that the above library websites also use this font.

46. Include Anchor Links for Important Links : An Anchor Link is a web link that allows the user to leapfrog to a specific point on a website page. Thus, the Anchor Links are used for important links. There were only 4 per cent of the library websites that did not include Anchor Links i.e. NITR.

47. Client Side Image Map : There were a significant 92 percent of the institutions that did not feature the Client

Side Images Map on their library websites. These institutions were IITK, IITR, IITB, NITR, IIMA, IITD, IITG, IISERP, IITBBS, THU, IITKG, IITM, ISBH, IMSC, SINP, NITT, NITK, IARI, JNCARS, IITH, IIITH, IISERK and TIRF. All these library websites need to feature in this vital aspect. The <map> tag is used to define a client-side image-map. The image-map is an image with clickable areas. The required name attribute of the <map> element is associated with the <img> use map attribute and creates a relationship between the image and the map. The <map> element contains a number of <area> elements that define the clickable areas in the image map.

48. Home Page Within 800 * 600 Pixels : There were 88 per cent of the library websites that did not have a home page within 800 * 600 pixels. This was applicable to the following institutions: IITK, IITR, IITB, NITR, IIMA, IITD, IITG, IISERP, IITBBS, THU, BITP, IITKG, ISBH, IMSC, SINP, NITT, NITK, IARI, IITH, IIITH, IISERK and TIRF. The average Website, Homepage dimension should be 800 * 600 pixels as they fit in the browser window without horizontal scrolling. Page height, width and alignment should be according to the design. This means that there is the creation of web pages that adapt to different devices and screen sizes. It uses the same content but presents it differently depending on whether it is the mobile phone, i-pad, laptop or desk top computer. The above library websites should essentially adhere to the above specifications.

49. Content of Pages Does Not Require Scrolling: Almost all the library websites have this feature of content of pages does not require scrolling. The institutions (96 percent) that have this feature were namely, IITK, IITR, IITB, NITR, IIMA, IITD, IITG, IISERP, IITBBS, THU, BITP, IITKG, ISBH, IMSC, SINP, NITT, NITC, NITK, IARI, JNCARS, IITH, IIITH, IISERK and TIRF. The content of the pages included information on the web page that included text, images and sound. Websites having long or infinite scrolling areas that leads to traversing across chunks of content without any interruption.

50. Sufficient Space for Links : All institutional library websites apparently had sufficient space for links. Sufficient space exists for links which help the user maintain a comfortable visual flow through the text. It also provides for adequate separation between elements in the layout.

51. Leave Space Between Letters of Abbreviation: There were 84 per cent of the library websites that did not have the provision to leave space between letters of abbreviations. The names of these institutions are, IITR, IITB, NITR, IIMA, IITD, IITG, IISERP, IITBBS, BITP, IITKG, IITM, ISBH, IMSC, NITC, NITK, IARI, JNCARS, IITH, IIITH, IISERK and TIRF. If the webmaster leave space between letters of abbreviation it would improve readability and increase the user's efficacy.

52. Limit Page to 200 kb of Graphics : There were 28 per cent of the library websites that did not limit page to 200 kb of graphics. The names of these institutions were IITR, IITB, IIMA, THU, BITP, NITT and NITC. Graphics should be limited in a page to 200 kb because larger graphics can overload a website and cause it to either crash and hang. The above mentioned library website should make this change with immediate effect.

53. Target-Main Arguments to Link to Tags : There were 36 per cent of the library websites that did not have the 'Target – Main Arguments to Link to Tag's. The institutions that did not have this feature are BITP, SINP, JNCARS, ISBH, IMSC, NITK, IITH, IIITH and IISERK. Links are used to move from one page to another and are seen as default set in blue underlined text. The search engines have a limited window which is known as "Target Main Argument" in which there are keywords. Links are used to move from place to place on the same page of a website. The above website should factor in this feature immediately.

54. Navigation Bars at the Bottom of the Page : There were 48 per cent of the institutional library websites that did not have the feature of Navigation Bars at the bottom of the page. These institutions were - IITK, IITR, NITR, IITD, BITP, IITKG, IIMSC, SINP, NITC, JNCARS, IISERK and TRIF. A Navigation Bar is a section of a graphic user interface intended to aid users in accessing information and therefore should necessarily added to the library website.

5.2.2. WATS Observations

The following is a discussion of the WATS scores for 25 institutions on various parameters. The scores have been segregated into three categories on the basis of placement on the graph.

Thus, the three categories that emerge are:

1. **High :** Having scores from 7 to 10
2. **Medium :** Having scores from 4 to 6.9
3. **Low :** Having scores from 0 to 3.9

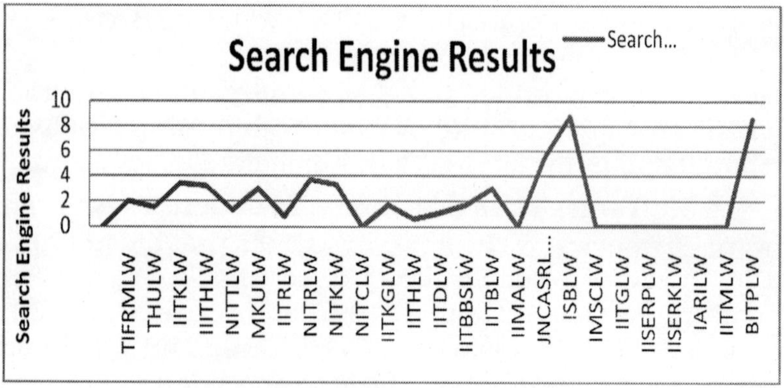

Fig. 5.1. Search Engine Results

Table 5.1. Search Engine Results

Level	*No. of Library Websites*	*Percent*	*Institutes*
High	2	8	ISB, BITP
Medium	1	4	JNCASR
Low	22	88	NITR, IITK, IITB, IITD, IITG, NITT, IMSC, THU, IIMA, NITK, TIFRM, IITR, IISERP, IIITH, IITKG, IITH, IISERK, IARI, MKU, IITBBS, NITC, IITM

In the WATS analysis several parameters were taken among which the first was about how a website appears in the results of a search engine like Google. In the 'High' category, which had 8 per cent of the library websites, were ISB and BITP. The 'Middle' category had the least institutional library websites or 4 per cent namely JNCASR. The 'Lowest' category had 88 per cent of the websites namely NITR, IITK, IITB, IITD, IITG, NITT, IMSC, THU, IIMA, NITK, TIFRM, IITR, IISERP, IIITH, IITKG, IITH, IISERK, IARI, MKU, IITBBS, NITC and IITM.

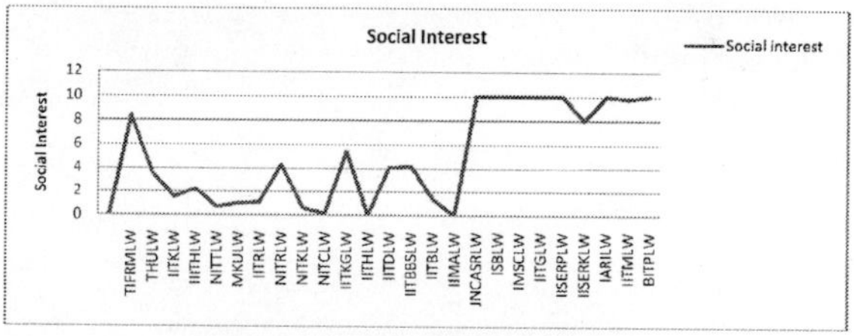

Fig. 5.2. Social Interest

Table 5.2. Social Interest

Level	*No. of Library Websites*	*Percent*	*Institutes*
High	10	40	ISB, IMSC, IITG, IISERP, IARI, BITP, IITM, TIFRM, IISERK, JNCASR
Medium	4	16	IITKG, NITR, IITBBS, IITD
Low	11	44	THU, IIITH, IITK, IITB, IITR, MKU, NITT, NITK, NITC, IITH, IIMA

The indicator on Social Interest examines the level of interest generated among viewers of a website for its individual pages. Among the websites that fell in the 'High' category were 40 per cent of the total number of institutional library websites examined and were namely, ISB, IMSC, IITG, IISERP, IARI, BITP, IITM, TIFRM, IISERK and JNCASR. There were 16 per cent who fell in the 'Middle' category and were namely IITKG, NITR, IITBBS and IITD. The 'Low' category institutional library websites were 44 per cent and comprised THU, IIITH, IITK, IITB, IITR, MKU, NITT, NITK, NITC, IITH and IIMA.

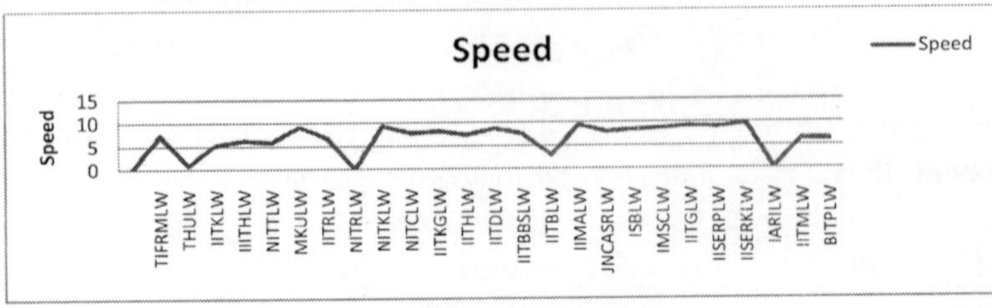

Fig. 5.3. Speed

Table 5.3. Speed

Level	*No. of Library Websites*	*Percent*	*Institutes*
High	15	60	IISERK, IIMA, NITK, IITG, MKU, IISERP, IITD, IMSC, ISB, IITKG, JNCASR, NIT, IITBBS, TIFRM, IITH
Medium	6	24	IITR, IITM, IIITH, BITP, NITT, IITK
Low	4	16	IITB, THU, IARI, NITR

The Speed indicator was a measure of the speed of the website and included factors like file size and application response time. There were 60 per cent of the institutes which had library websites in the 'High' category and they were namely IISERK, IIMA, NITK, IITG, MKU, IISERP, IITD, IMSC, ISB, IITKG, JNCASR, NIT, IITBBS,

TIFRM and IITH. There were 24 per cent in the 'Middle' category namely IITR, IITM, IIITH, BITP, NITT and IITK. There were just 16 per cent in the 'Low' category namely IITB, THU, IARI and NITR.

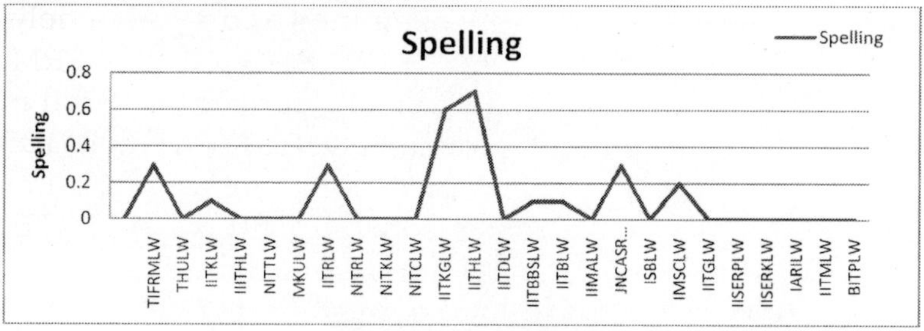

Fig. 5.4. Spelling

Table 5.4. Spelling

Level	***No. of Library Websites***	***Percent***	***Institutes***
Low	25	100	IITH, IITKG, TIFRM, IIT, JNCASR, IMSC, IITK, IITBBS, IITB, THU, IIITH, NITT, MKU, NITR, NITK, NITC, IITD, IIMA, ISB, IITG, IISER, IISERK, IARI, IITM, BITP.

The 'Spelling' indicator reflected upon the fact that if there were spelling's errors in the text used in the website content it would have a detrimental impact. It would also make the website difficult to comprehend. It was most disappointing to say that 100 per cent of the websites lay in the 'Low' category. That is all websites had poor spelling's accuracy in their content.

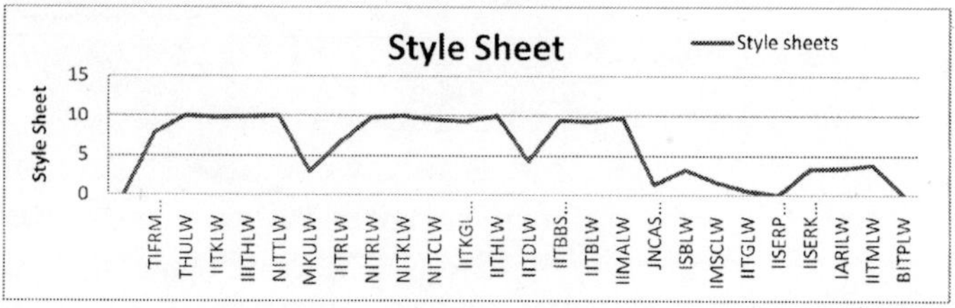

Fig. 5.5. Style Sheet

Table 5.5. Style Sheets

Level	*No. of Library Websites*	*Percent*	*Institutes*
High	13	52	THU, NITT, NITK, IITH, IIITH, IITK, NITR, IIMA, NITC, IITBBS, IITKG, IITB, TIFRM
Medium	3	12	IITR, IITD, IITM
Low	9	36	IARI, IISERK, ISB, MKU, IMSC, JNCASR, IITG, IISERP, BITP

There was the indicator of style sheets wherein Cascading Style Sheets (CSS) denoted a standard means of building up web pages. This indicator determined whether the web pages had been built using the CSS. The findings showed that 52 per cent of the institutional library websites belonged to the 'High' category and were THU, NITT, NITK, IITH, IIITH, IITK, NITR, IIMA, NITC, IITBBS, IITKG, IITB and TIFRM. While 12 per cent belonged to the 'Middle' category and were namely IITR, IITD and IITM. There were 36 per cent of the institutional library websites that fell in the 'Low' category and were namely IARI, IISERK, ISB, MKU, IMSC, JNCASR, IITG, IISERP and BITP.

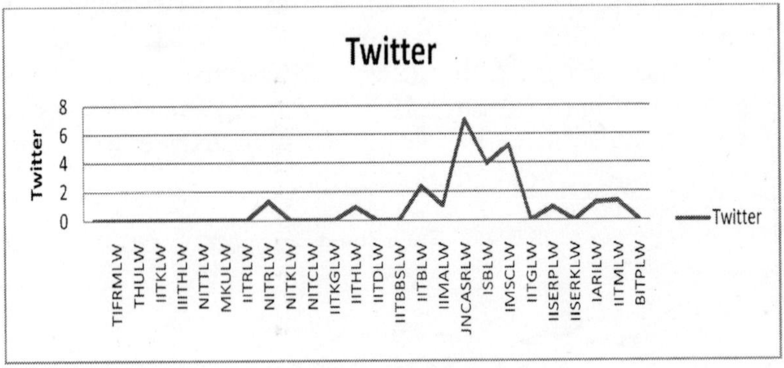

Fig. 5.6. Twitter

Table 5.6. Twitter

Level	*No. of Library Websites*	*Percent*	*Institutes*
High	1	4	JNCASR
Medium	1	4	IMSC
Low	23	92	ISB, IITB, NITR, IITM, IARI, IIMA, IITH, IISERP, TIFRM, THU, IITK, IIITH, NITT, MKU, IITR, NITK, NITC, IITKG, IITD, IITBBS, IITG, IISERK, BITP

Whether the websites were linked to a Twitter account or not was determined by this indicator. It was also observed that the frequency of usage of Twitter was also a determinant of the quality of the website. Under this indicator there were only four per cent that fell in the 'High' category, namely, JNCASR. Another four per cent fell in the 'Medium' category and were namely, IMSC. There were 92 per cent that did not have this feature. They were namely ISB, IITB, NITR, IITM, IARI, IIMA, IITH, IISERP, TIFRM, THU, IITK, IIITH, NITT, MKU, IITR, NITK, NITC, IITKG, IITD, IITBBS, IITG, IISERK and BITP.

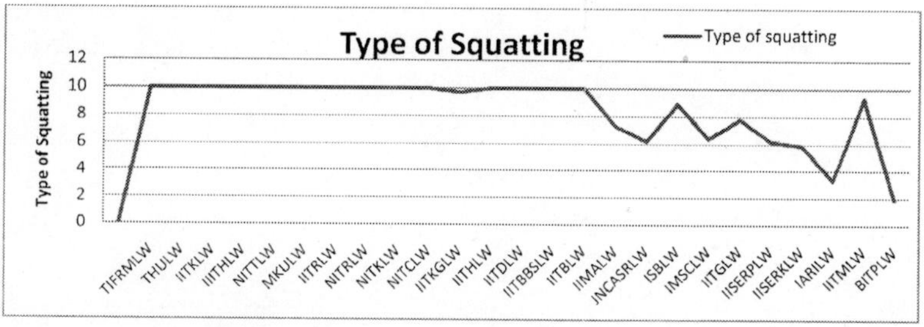

Fig. 5.7. Type of Squatting

Table 5.7. Type of Squatting

Level	*No. of Library Websites*	*Percent*	*Institutes*
High	19	76	TIFRM, THU, IITK, IIITH, NITT, MKU, IITR, NITR, NITK, NITC, IITH, IITD, IITBBS, IITB, IITKG, IITM, ISB, IITG, IIMA
Medium	5	20	IMSC, JNCASR, IISERP, IISERK, IARI
Low	1	4	BITP

The feature on websites that tests if the variations or typos of the domain name have been registered are known as Typosquatting. The institutional library websites which fell in the 'High' category were 76 per cent and are TIFRM, THU, IITK, IIITH, NITT, MKU, IITR, NITR, NITK, NITC, IITH, IITD, IITBBS, IITB, IITKG, IITM, ISB, IITG and IIMA. There were also 20 per cent of the library websites that fell in the 'Medium' category. These were IMSC, JNCASR, IISERP, IISERK and IARI. There were only four per cent of the websites in the 'Low' category, namely BITP.

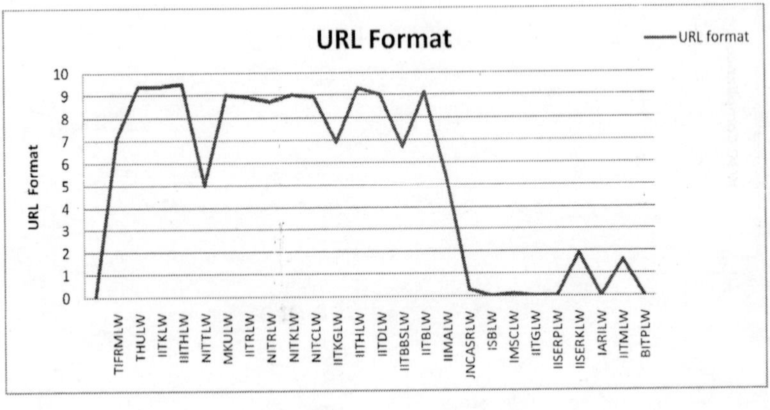

Fig. 5.8. URL Format

Table 5.8. URL Format

Level	*No. of Library Websites*	*Percent*	*Institutes*
High	12	48	IIITH, THU, IITK, IITH, IITB, MKU, NITK, IITD, IITR, NITC, NITR, TIFRM
Medium	4	16	IITKG, IITBBS, IIMA, NITT
Low	9	36	IISERK, IITM, JNCASR, IMSC, ISB, IITG, IISERP, IARI, BITP

The URL is the web address and the URL format is a test of whether the URLs work when fragments are chopped off. It is very common among users because www.example.com/news/articles1 tends to become www.example.com/news/. Regarding this feature 48 per cent of the websites were in the 'High' category namely IIITH, THU, IITK, IITH, IITB, MKU, NITK, IITD, IITR, NITC, NITR and TIFRM. There were also 16 per cent in the middle category namely IITKG, IITBBS, IIMA and NITT. There were 36 per cent in the 'Low' category namely IISERK, IITM, JNCASR, IMSC, ISB, IITG, IISERP, IARI and BITP.

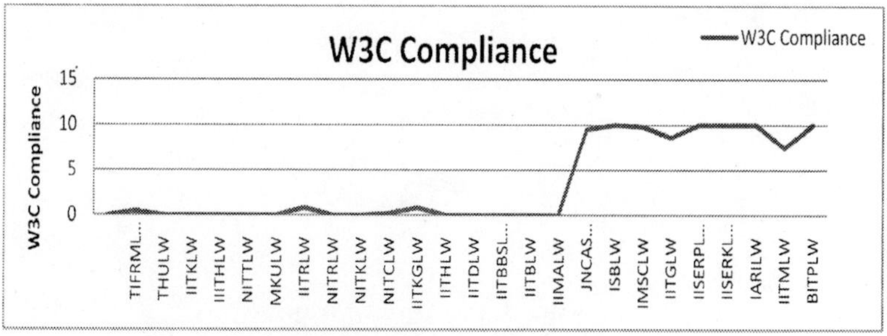

Fig. 5.9. W3C Compliance

Table 5.9. W3C Compliance

Level	*No. of Library Websites*	*Percent*	*Institutes*
High	9	36	ISB, IMS, IITG, IISERP, IISERK, IARI, IITM, BITP, JNCASR
Low	16	64	IITB, IITK, IITD, TIFRM, IITKG, IITR, NITR, IIITH, NITC, IITH, IIMA, NITK, IITBBS, THU, SINPL, NITT

The W3C Compliance tends to test whether the website is W3C Compliant. W3C is the primary standard body for the web. It defines the precise specifications of how the HTML or XHTML of a website should be written to ensure compatibility, accessibility and the following of best practices. The observed websites that fell in the 'High' category were 36 per cent and comprised ISB, IMS, IITG, IISERP, IISERK, IARI, IITM, BITP and JNCASR. The majority, that is 64 percent were placed in the 'Low' and were IITB, IITK, IITD, TIFRM, IITKG, IITR, NITR, IIITH, NITC, IITH, IIMA, NITK, IITBBS, THU, SINPL and NITT.

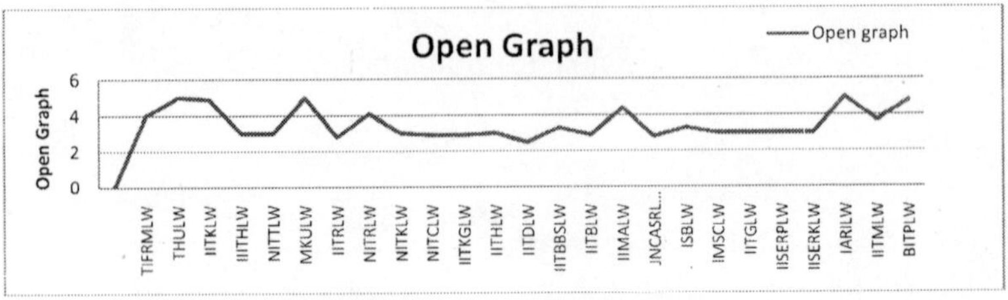

Fig. 5.10. Open Graph

Table 5.10. Open Graph

Level	*No. of Library Websites*	*Percent*	*Institutes*
Medium	9	36	THU, MKU, IARI, IITK, BITP, IIMA, NITR, TIFRM, IITM
Low	16	64	IITBBS, ISB, IIITH, NITT, NITK, IITH, IMSC, IITG, IISERP, IISERK, NITC, IITKG, IITB, IITR, JNCASR, IITD

The Open Graph feature on the website looks at how the website appears when it is shared on the social networking sites like Facebook and Twitter. None of the websites featured in the 'High' category. In the 'Middle' category were 36 per cent and were THU, MKU, IARI, IITK, BITP, IIMA, NITR, TIFRM and IITM. There were 64 per cent in the 'Low' category namely IITBBS, ISB, IIITH, NITT, NITK, IITH, IMSC, IITG, IISERP, IISERK, NITC, IITKG, IITB, IITR, JNCASR and IITD.

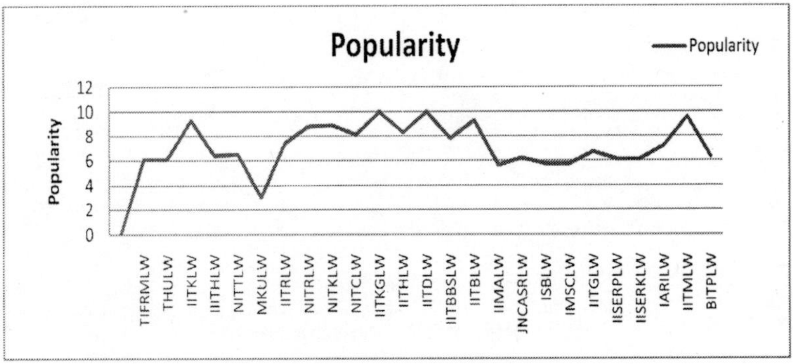

Fig. 5.11. Popularity

Table 5.11. Popularity

Level	*No. of Library Websites*	*Percent*	*Institutes*
High	12	48	IITKG, IITD, IITM, IITK, IITB, NITK, NITR, IITH, NITC, IITBBS, IITR, IARI
Medium	12	48	IITG, NITT, IIITH, BITP, JNCASR, TIFRM, THU, IISERP, IISERK, ISB, IMSC, IIMA
Low	1	4	MKU

The Popularity feature tests how popular is the website among the users. This property was seen in 48 per cent of the 'High' category websites namely IITKG, IITD, IITM, IITK, IITB, NITK, NITR, IITH, NITC, IITBBS, IITR and IARI. There were another 48 per cent that featured in the 'Middle' category and were namely IITG, NITT, IIITH, BITP, JNCASR, TIFRM, THU, IISERP, IISERK, ISB, IMSC and IIMA and those that were placed in the 'Low' category were 4 per cent and included MKU.

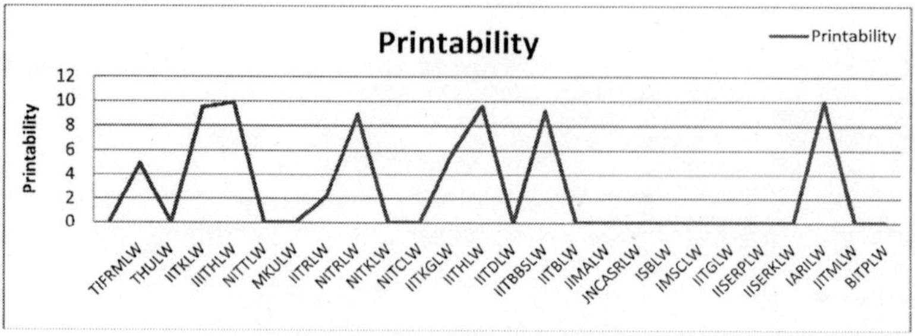

Fig. 5.12. Printability

Table 5.12. Printability

Level	*No. of Library Websites*	*Percent*	*Institutes*
High	6	24	IARI, IIITH, IITH, IITK, IITBBS, NITR
Medium	2	8	IITKG, TIFRM
Low	17	68	IITR, THU, NITT, MKU, NITK, NITC, IITD, IITB, IIMA, JNCASR, ISB, IMSC, IITG, IISERP, IISERK, IITM, BITP

The Printability property of the websites ensured whether or not the pages were designed for printing and showed how the homeapage appears when it is printed. There were 24 per cent of the library websites in the 'High' category and were namely IARI, IIITH, IITH, IITK, IITBBS and NITR. There were 8 per cent that featured in the 'Medium' category and were namely IITKG and TIFRM. There were 68 per cent of the websites that featured in the 'Low' category namely IITR, THU, NITT, MKU, NITK, NITC, IITD, IITB, IIMA, JNCASR, ISB, IMSC, IITG, IISERP, IISERK, IITM and BITP.

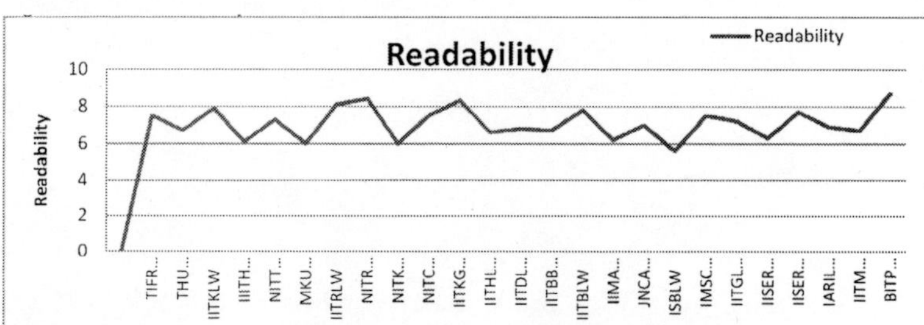

Fig. 5.13. Readability

Table 5.13. Readability

Level	*No. of Library Websites*	*Percent*	*Institutes*
High	13	52	BITP, NITR, IITKG, IITR, IITK, IITB, IISERK, TIFRM, NITC, IMSC, NITT, IITG, JNCASR
Medium	12	48	IARI, IITD, THU, IITBBS, IITM, IITH, IISERP, IIMA, IIITH, MKU, NITK, ISB

The Readability feature was a measure of legibility or how easily readable was the information given on the website. There were 52 percent of the websites that featured on the 'High' category namely BITP, NITR, IITKG, IITR, IITK, IITB, IISERK, TIFRM, NITC, IMSC, NITT, IITG and JNCASR. There were 48 percent of Library Websites that featured on Medium category namely IARI, IITD, THU, IITBBS, IITM, IITH, IISERP, IIMA, IIITH, MKU, NITK and ISB. There was no website that was in the 'Low' category.

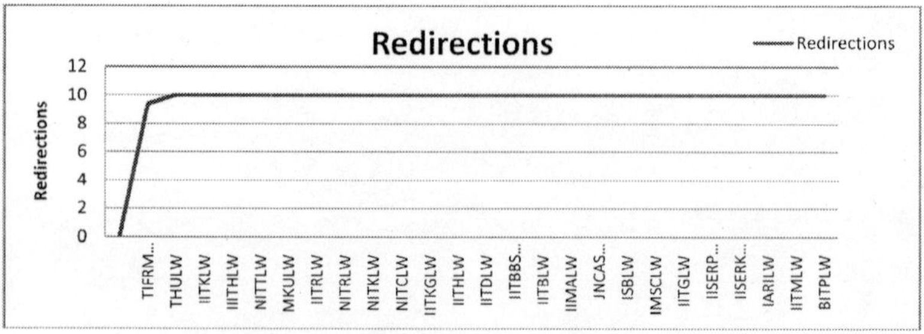

Fig. 5.14. Redirections

Table 5.14. Redirections

Level	*No. of Library Websites*	*Percent*	*Institutes*
High	25	100	THU, IITK, IIITH, NITT, MKU, IITR, NITR, NITK, NITC, IITKG, IITH, IITD, IITBBS, IITB, IIMA, JNCASR, ISB, IMSC, IITG, IISERP, IISERK, IARI, IITM, BITP, TIFRM

The Redirection feature of the website tests if the website uses the client side redirections and tends to prevent visitors from using the back button. All the websites were placed in the 'High' category in this regard. Thus, all the 25 websites observed and carried the redirections property THU, IITK, IIITH, NITT, MKU, IITR, NITR, NITK, NITC, IITKG, IITH, IITD, IITBBS, IITB, IIMA, JNCASR, ISB, IMSC, IITG, IISERP, IISERK, IARI, IITM, BITP and TIFRM.

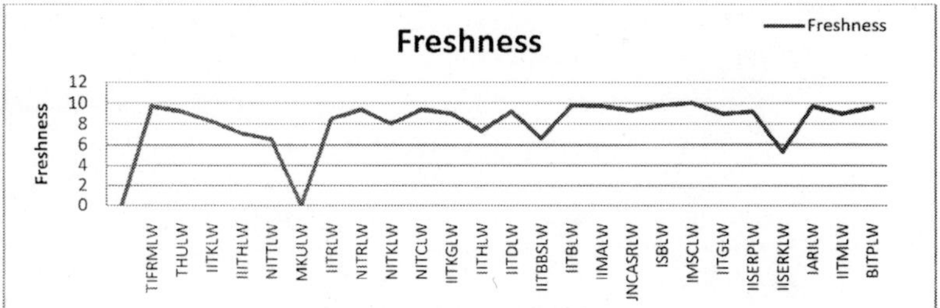

Fig. 5.15. Freshness

Table 5.15. Freshness

Level	*No. of Library Websites*	*Percent*	*Institutes*
High	21	84	MKU, IMSC, IITB, ISB, TIFRM, IIMA, IARI, BITP, NITR, NITC, JNCASR, THU, IITD, IISERP, IITKG, IITG,

			IITM, IITR, IITK, NITK, IITH
Medium	3	12	IIITH, IITBBS, NITT
Low	1	4	IISERK

The Freshness test determined how frequently the website was kept up to date and fresh. Also whether it was subsequently updated. A majority of the websites, that is, 84 percent were placed in the 'High' category and comprised MKU, IMSC, IITB, ISB, TIFRM, IIMA, IARI, BITP, NITR, NITC, JNCASR, THU, IITD, IISERP, IITKG, IITG, IITM, IITR, IITK, NITK and IITH. There were also 12 per cent of the library websites that were placed in the 'Middle' category and comprised IIITH, IITBBS and NITT while four per cent were in the 'Low' category and comprised only IISERK.

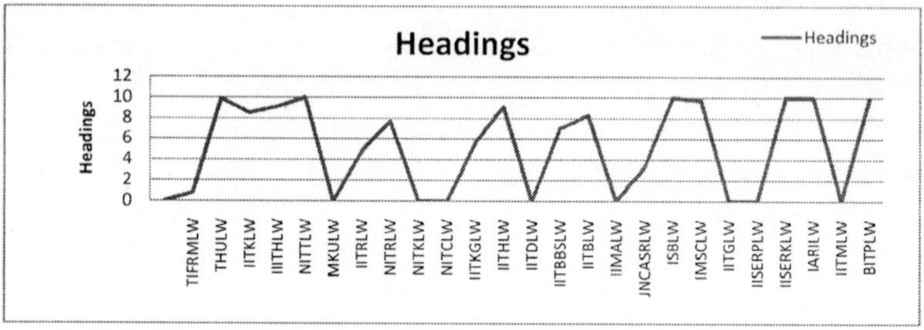

Fig. 5.16. Headings

Table 5.16. Headings

Level	*No. of Library Websites*	*Percent*	*Institutes*
High	13	52	NITT, ISB, IISERK, IARI, THU, BITP, IMSC, IIITH, IITH, IITK, IITB, NITR, IITBBS
Medium	2	8	IITKG, IITR
Low	10	40	JNCASR, TIFRM, MKU, NITK, NITC, IITD, IIMA, IITG, IISERP, IITM

The Headings feature tested whether the defined

headings were aptly defined and used adequately in the websites to list off descriptive features. A good use of headings has a positive effect on the search engine rankings given by users.

There were 52 per cent of the institutional library websites in the 'High' category, namely NITT, ISB, IISERK, IARI, THU, BITP, IMSC, IIITH, IITH, IITK, IITB, NITR, IITBBS and 8 per cent that were in the 'Middle' category namely IITKG and IITR. There were also 40 per cent of the websites that were placed in the 'Low' category and comprised JNCASR, TIFRM, MKU, NITK, NITC, IITD, IIMA, IITG, IISERP and IITM.

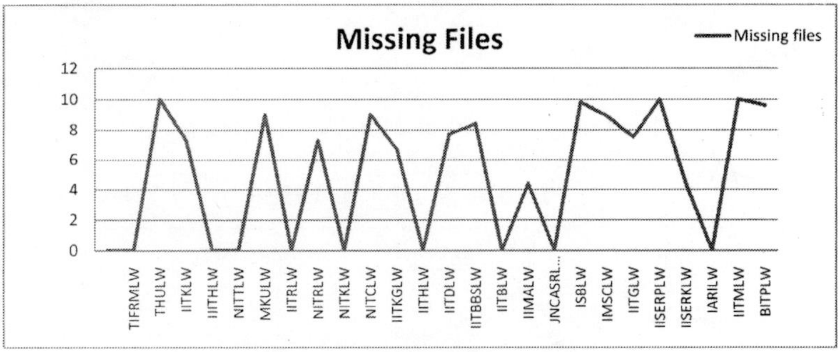

Fig. 5.17. Missing Files

Table 5.17. Missing Files

Level	*No. of Library Websites*	*Percent*	*Institutes*
High	13	52	THU, IISERP, IITM, ISB, BITP, MKU, NITC, IMSC, IITBBS, IITD, IITG, IITK, NITR
Medium	3	12	IITKG, IIMA, IISERK
Low	9	36	TIFRM, IIITH, NITT, IITR, NITK, IITH, IITB, JNCASR, IARI

The Missing Files feature detects the missing files within a website. There are 52 per cent of the institutional library websites that were placed in the 'High' category and were THU, IISERP, IITM, ISB, BITP, MKU, NITC, IMSC, IITBBS, IITD, IITG, IITK and NITR. There were 12 per cent that were placed in the 'Medium' category and were IITKG, IIMA and IISERK. There were also 36 per cent that featured in the 'Low' category and included TIFRM, IIITH, NITT, IITR, NITK, IITH, IITB, JNCASR and IARI.

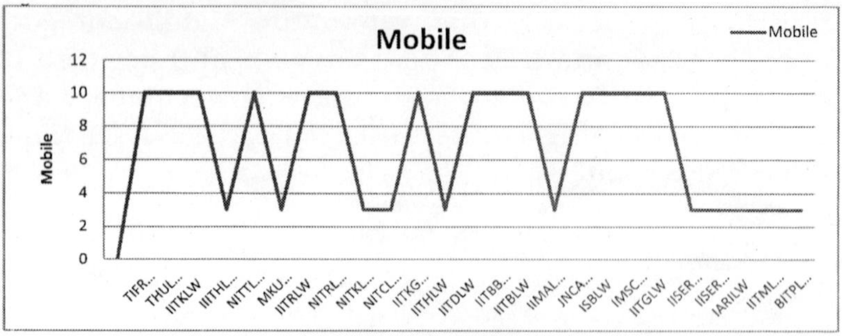

Fig. 5.18. Mobile

Table 5.18. Mobile

Level	***No. of Library Websites***	***Percent***	***Institutes***
High	14	56	TIFRM, THU, IITK, NITT, IITR, NITR, IITKG, IITD, IITBBS, IITB, JNCASR, ISB, IMSC, IITG
Low	11	44	IIITH, MKU, NITK, NITC, IITH, IIMA, IISERP, IISERK, IARI, IITM, BITP

The Mobile feature tests whether a website is optimized for mobile and tablet devices. The websites were observed to lie in the 'High' and 'Low' categories totally. There was no 'Middle' category. There were 56 per cent that were in the 'High' category and comprised TIFRM, THU, IITK, NITT, IITR, NITR, IITKG, IITD, IITBBS, IITB, JNCASR, ISB, IMSC and IITG. There was another 44 per cent that was placed in the 'Low' category namely IIITH,

MKU, NITK, NITC, IITH, IIMA, IISERP, IISERK, IARI, IITM and BITP.

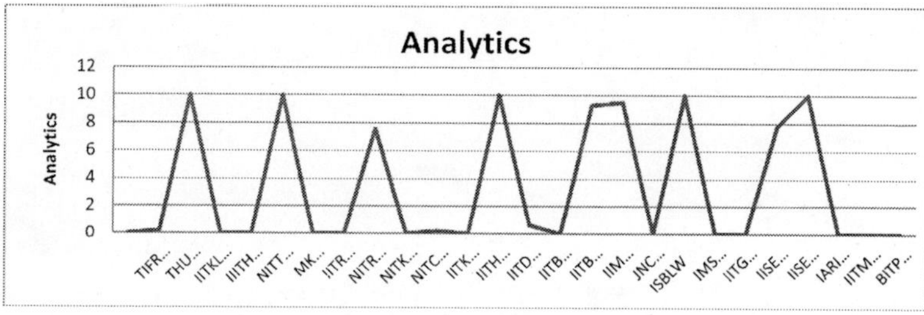

Fig. 5.19. Analytics

Table 5.19. Analytics

Level	*No. of Library Websites*	*Percent*	*Institutes*
High	9	36	THU, NITT, ISB, IITH, IISERK, IIMA, IITB, IISERP, NITR
Low	16	64	IITD, TIFRM, NITC, NITK, MKU, JNCASR, IMSC, IITR, IITM, IITK, IITKG, IITG, IITBBS, IIITH, IARI, BITP

The Analytics feature allows for a detailed analysis of user behavior. The observed websites were seen to fall only in the 'High' and 'Low' categories. There were 36 per cent that were placed in 'High' category and were THU, NITT, ISB, IITH, IISERK, IIMA, IITB, IISERP and NITR. There were 64 per cent that were placed in the 'Low' category and comprised IITD, TIFRM, NITC, NITK, MKU, JNCASR, IMSC, IITR, IITM, IITK, IITKG, IITG, IITBBS, IIITH, IARI and BITP.

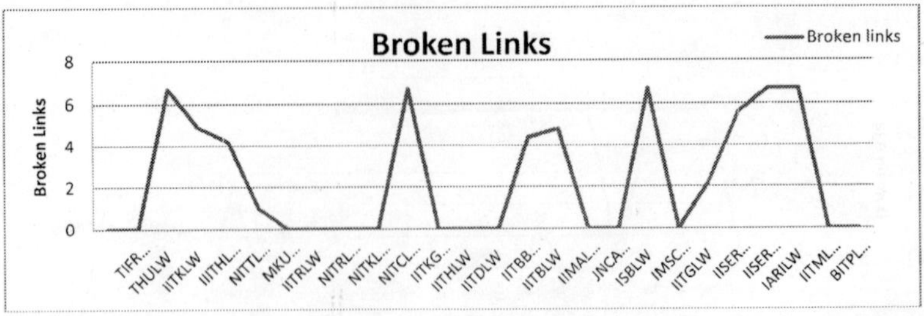

Fig. 5.20. Broken Links

Table 5.20. Broken Links

Level	***No. of Library Websites***	***Percent***	***Institutes***
Medium	10	40	THU, NITC, ISB, IISERK, IARI, IISERP,IITK, IITB, IITBBS, IIITH
Low	15	60	IITG, NITT, TIFRM, NITR, NITK, MKU, JNCASR, IMSC, IITR, IITM, IITKG, IITH, IITD, IIMA, BITP

The Broken Links feature comprised those links to web addresses that either were showed errors. There were maximum numbers of websites that were placed in the 'Low' category and were namely IITG, NITT, TIFRM, NITR, NITK, MKU, JNCASR, IMSC, IITR, IITM, IITKG, IITH, IITD, IIMA and BITP. There were 40 percent of the institutional library websites that were placed in the 'Middle' category. These were THU, NITC, ISB, IISERK, IARI, IISERP, IITK, IITB, IITBBS and IIITH.

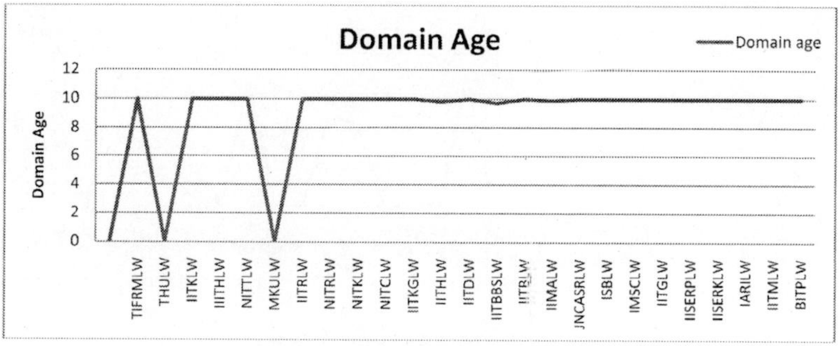

Fig. 5.21. Domain Age

Table 5.21. Domain Age

Level	*No. of Library Websites*	*Percent*	*Institutes*
High	23	92	TIFRM, IITK, IIITH, NITT, IITR, NITR, NITK, NITC, IITKG, IITD, IITB, JNCASR, ISB, IMSC, IITG, IISERP, IISERK, IARI, IITM, BITP, IIMA, IITH, IITBBS
Low	2	8	THU, MKU

The Domain Age depicts the trust of a website. There were maximum number that is 92 per cent of the websites that featured in the 'High' category and were TIFRM, IITK, IIITH, NITT, IITR, NITR, NITK, NITC, IITKG, IITD, IITB, JNCASR, ISB, IMSC, IITG, IISERP, IISERK, IARI, IITM, BITP, IIMA, IITH and IITBBS while 8 per cent featured in the 'Low' category and were THU and MKU. There were none that could be placed in the 'Middle' level.

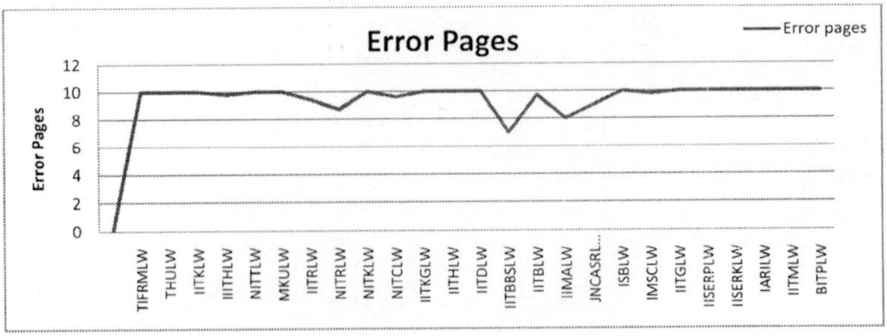

Fig. 5.22. Error Pages

Table 5.22. Error Pages

Level	*No. of Library Websites*	*Percent*	*Institutes*
High	25	100	ISB, IISERK, BITP, IITH, IITK, IITKG, THU, TIFRM, IARI, NITT, ISERP, IITG, NITK, IITM, IITD, MKU, IMSC, IIITH, IITB, NITC, IITR, JNCASR, NITR, IIMA, ITBBS

Error Pages checked for error messages and faults of the websites. This feature was available in all the websites participating in the study. There were no 'Middle' or 'Low' level categories.

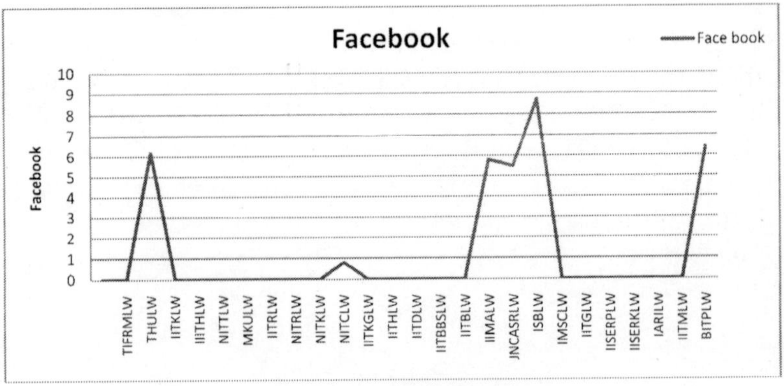

Fig. 5.23. Facebook

Table 5.23. Facebook

Level	*No. of Library Websites*	*Percent*	*Institutes*
High	1	4	ISB
Medium	4	16	BITP, THU, IIMA, JNCASR
Low	20	80	NITC, TIFRM, NITT, NITR, NITK, MKU, IMSC, IITR, IITM, IITK, IITKG, IITH, IITG, IITD, IITB, IITBBS, IISERP, IISERK, IIITH, IARI

Facebook was an indicator of whether the website had a Facebook page. There were 'High' category websites namely ISB which comprised 4 per cent and the 'Middle' level websites were 16 per cent and comprised BITP, THU, IIMA and JNCASR. There was also the 'Low' category which featured 80 per cent of the websites namely NITC, TIFRM, NITT, NITR, NITK, MKU, IMSC, IITR, IITM, IITK, IITKG, IITH, IITG, IITD, IITB, IITBBS, IISERP, IISERK, IIITH and IARI.

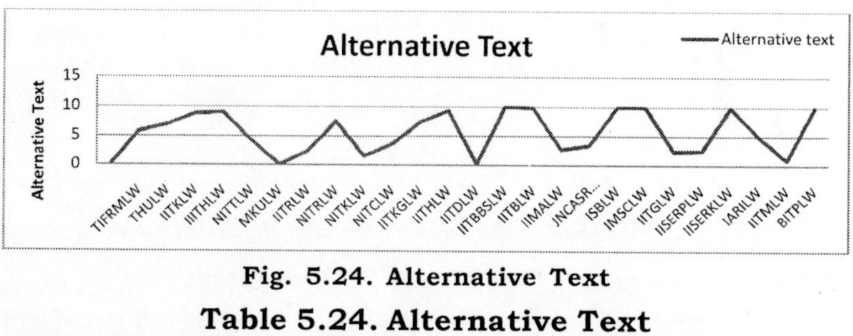

Fig. 5.24. Alternative Text

Table 5.24. Alternative Text

Level	*No. of Library Websites*	*Percent*	*Institutes*
High	11	44	ISB, IITBBS, IMSC, IISERK, BITP, IITB, IITH, IIITH, IITK, NITR, IITKG
Medium	4	16	THU, TIFRM, IARI, NITT

Low	10	40	NITC, JNCASR, IIMA, IISERP, IITR, IITG, NITK, IITM, IITD, MKU

The Alternative Text depicts the type of images that are contained in the website. There were 44 per cent of the websites in the 'High' category and comprised ISB, IITBBS, IMSC, IISERK, BITP, IITB, IITH, IIITH, IITK, NITR and IITKG. There were 16 per cent of the websites in the 'Middle' category and comprised THU, TIFRM, IARI and NITT. There were also 40 in the 'Low' category namely NITC, JNCASR, IIMA, IISERP, IITR, IITG, NITK, IITM, IITD and MKU.

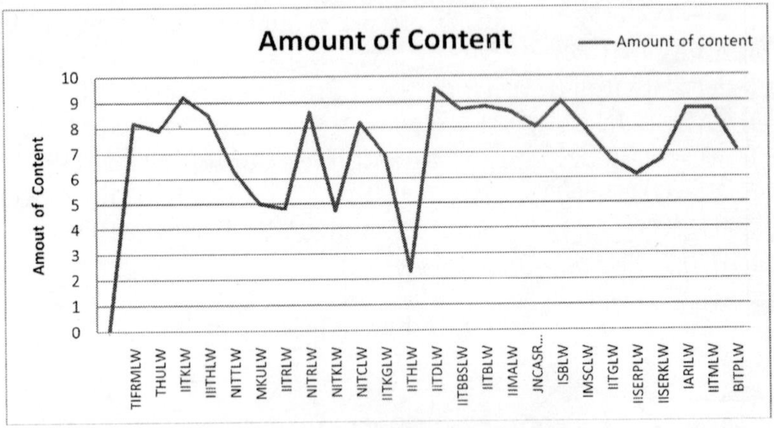

Fig. 5.25. Amount of Content

Table 5.25. Amount of Content

Level	***No. of Library Websites***	***Percent***	***Institutes***
High	13	52	IITD, IITK, ISB, IITB, IITM, IITBBS, IARI, NITR, IIMA, IIITH, TIFRM, NITC, JNCASR
Medium	11	44	THU, IMSC, BITP, IITKG, IITG, IISERK, NITT, IISERP, MKU, IITR, NITK
Low	1	4	IITH

The Amount of Content is a measure of the text content of a website. The measurement is done in terms of word count. The institutional library websites that fell in the 'High' category featured 52 per cent and were namely IITD, IITK, ISB, IITB, IITM, IITBBS, IARI, NITR, IIMA, IIITH, TIFRM, NITC and JNCASR. There were 44 per cent that featured in the 'Middle' category and comprised THU, IMSC, BITP, IITKG, IITG, IISERK, NITT, IISERP, MKU, IITR and NITK. There were only 4 per cent in the 'Low' category i.e. IITH library website.

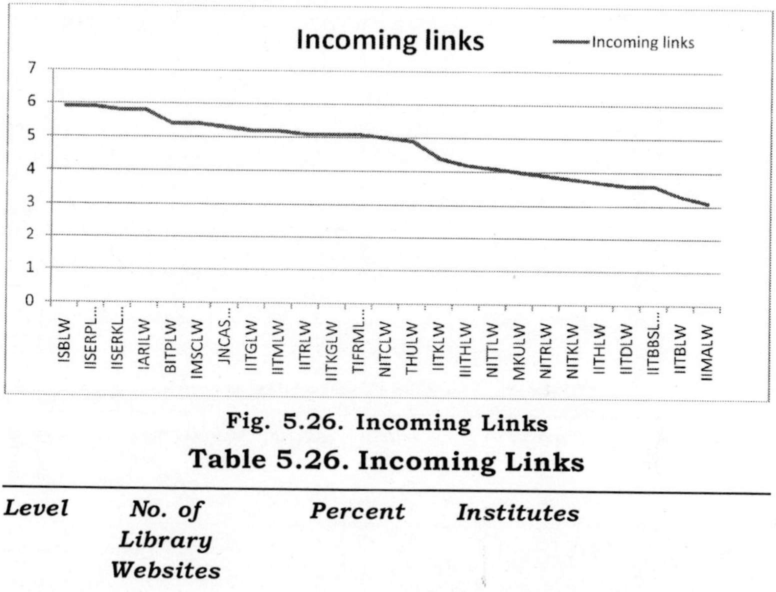

Fig. 5.26. Incoming Links

Table 5.26. Incoming Links

Level	*No. of Library Websites*	*Percent*	*Institutes*
Medium	18	72	ISB, IISERP, IISERK, IARI, BITP, IMSC, JNCASR, IITG, IITM, IITR, IITKG, TIFRM, NITC, THU, IITK, IIITH, NITT, MKU
Low	7	28	NITR, NITK, IITH, IITD, IITBBS, IITB, IIMA

The Incoming Links that pointed towards particular websites and compared them against other sites. The website that has many links had a higher score. There were no websites that featured in the 'High' category while the 'Middle' category had 72 per cent websites namely ISB, IISERP, IISERK, IARI, BITP, IMSC, JNCASR, IITG, IITM, IITR, IITKG, TIFRM, NITC, THU, IITK, IIITH, NITT and MKU. There were 28 per cent of the websites in the 'Low' category namely NITR, NITK, IITH, IITD, IITBBS, IITB and IIMA.

5.2.3. Web Impact Factor (WIF), Revised Web Impact Factor (RWIF), Overall Web Impact Factor (OWIF) Observations

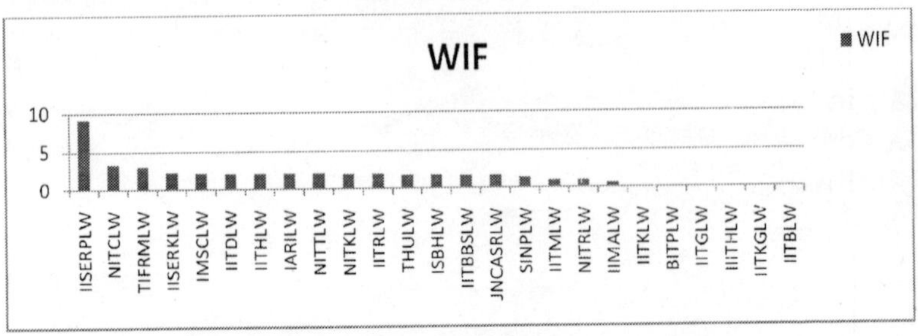

Fig. 5.27. WIF

Table 5.27. Performance on WIF

WIF	*Range*	*No. of Library Websites*	*%age*	*Institutes*
High	More Than 1	18	72	IISERP, NITC, TIFRM, IISERK, IMSC, IITD, IITH, IARI, NITT, NITK, IITR, THU, ISBH, IITBBS, JNCASR, SINP, IITM, NITR.
Medium	Between 0.5 to 1	01	4	IIMA
Low	Below 0.5	06	24	IITK, BITP, IITG, IIITH, IITKG, IITB

Library Websites of Research and Technical institutions of India were then ranked as 'low', 'medium' and 'high' range on the scale of WIF. The findings showed that the institution's library websites ranging in the less than 0.5 category would be in the 'low' category while those ranging from 0.5 to 01 ranged in the 'middle' category and the ones ranging above 1 were considered in the 'high' category.

Thus, the spread of the institutional library websites has been placed in the following categories. There were 72 per cent of the library websites in the 'high' category, 4 per cent in the 'middle' category and 24 per cent in the 'low' category. The institutional library websites that were in the 'High' category are IISERP, NITC, TIFRM, IISERK, IMSC, IITD, IITH, IARI, NITT, NITK, IITR, THU, ISBH, IITBBS, JNCASR, SINP, IITM and NITR. The one that was in the 'Middle' category are IIMA and those in the 'Low' category are IITK, BITP, IITG, IIITH, IITKG and IITB. This has been depicted in Table No. 5.27.

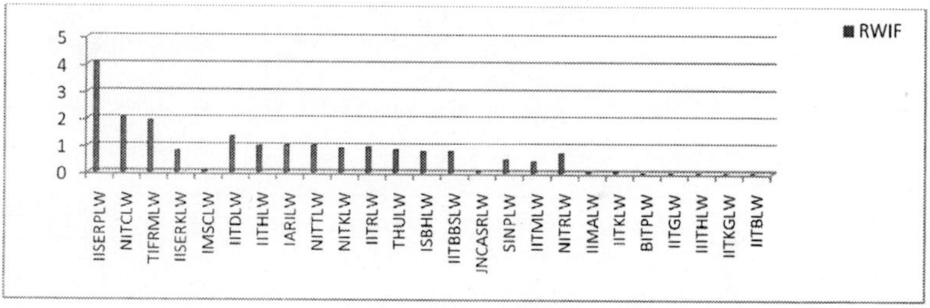

Fig. 5.28. RWIF

Table 5.28. Performance on RWIF

WIF	*Range*	*No. of Library Websites*	*%age*	*Institutes*
High	More Than 1	06	24	IISERP, NITC, TIFRM, IITD, IARI, NITT
Medium	Between 1 to 0.5	08	32	IITH, NITR, IISERK, NITK, IITR, THU, ISBH, IITBBS
Low	Below 0.5	11	44	JNCASR, SINP, IITM, , IMSC, IIMA, IITK, BITP, IITG, IIITH, IITKG, IITB

On the RWIF analysis the 'Low' range of institutional library websites were those that were below 0.5 and had 44 per cent of the library websites namely JNCASR, SINP, IITM, IMSC, IIMA, IITK, BITP, IITG, IIITH, IITKG and IITB. The 'Middle' range of 0.5 to 1 had 32 percent of the websites namely IITH, NITR, IISERK, NITK, IITR, THU, ISBH and IITBBS. There were also the 'High' or more than 1 category range. The percentage of these libraries is 32 per cent and they are namely IISERP, NITC, TIFRM, IITD, IARI and NITT.

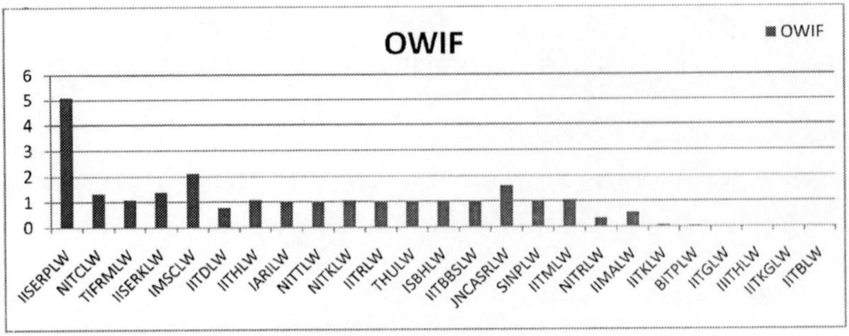

Fig. 5.29. OWIF

Table 5.29. Performance on OWIF

OWIF	***Range***	***No. of Library Websites***	***%age***	***Institutes***
High	More Than 1	14	56	IISERP, NITC, TIFRM, IISERK, IMSC, IITH, IARI, NITT, NITK, ISBH, IITBBS, JNCASR, SINP, IITM,
Medium	Between 1 to 0.5	04	16	IITD, IITR, THU, IIMA
Low	Below 0.5	07	28	IITK, BITP, IITG, IIITH, IITKG, IITB, NITR

The OWIF ranges have also been segregated into 'Low' which formed 28 per cent in terms of institutional library websites namely IITK, BITP, IITG, IIITH, IITKG, IITB and NITR. Then there were the 'Middle' category library websites namely IITD, IITR, THU and IIMA. The

'High' level institutional library websites were IISERP, NITC, TIFRM, IISERK, IMSC, IITH, IARI, NITT, NITK, ISBH, IITBBS, JNCASR, SINP and IITM .

5.2.4. Ranking on the basis of Composite and Institutional Placement

On the basis of the scores of WI, WA, WIF, RWIF and OWIF all the institutional library websites were ranked and a comparison was made with their ranking as per Composite Ranks. In some cases there has been a total turn about as far as composite and institutional ranking goes. For example ISBHLW has a Composite Rank (CR) of 1 but an Institutional Rank (IR) of 20. Similarly THULW showed a CR of 5 against an IR of 14; IITBBSLW had a Composite Ranks of 6 juxtaposed with an IR of 25 and IISERPLW has a Composite Rank of 8 against Institutional Ranking of 23.

Contrarily IITMLW had a CR of 22 and an 1R of 3. Similarly, TIFRMLW had a CR of 24 poised against an IR of 5. The only institutional website that had retained the CR and IR position of 18 was IARILW followed closely by NITKLW which had a CR score position of 25 and an IR score position of 24. Table No. 5.30 shows the details of the institutional website positions.

5.2.5. Summary

IIT Roorkee Library Website (78 score) scored first position in Web Indicators Ranking followed by IIT Kanpur Library Website (69) at second position and IIT Bombay Library Website (68), IIM Ahmedabad Library Website (68), NIT Rourkela Library Website (68) together at the third position. Last position was scored by the Tata Institute of Fundamental Research, Mumbai Library Website obtaining 37 out of the total score of 105. Mean, Median and Standard Deviation scores of Web Indicators on library websites are 52.32, 54 and 9.97.

Table 5.30. Composite Rank (CR) of Research & Technical Institution Library Websites (R&TILWS)

Sr.	*R&T ILW*	*WI*	*WA*	*WIF*	*RWIF*	*OWIF*	*Mean Score*	*Total*	*Composite Rank*	*Institutional Rank*
1	ISBHLW	55	187.5	1.783	0.767	1.016	49.2	246.1	1	20
2	IITKLW	69	161.6	0.132	0.0722	0.06	46.2	230.9	2	2
3	NITRLW	68	159	1.040	0.703	0.337	45.8	229.1	3	9
4	IITBLW	68	153.9	0.0003	0.0001	0.0001	44.4	221.9	4	1
5	THULW	59	154.9	1.814	0.829	0.985	43.5	217.5	5	14
6	IITBBSLW	59	151.6	1.773	0.773	1	42.8	214.1	6	25
7	IITKGLW	58	150	0.0004	0.0001	0.0002	41.6	208.0	8	6
8	IISERPLW	59	130.6	9.182	4.062	5.119	41.6	208.0	8	23
9	IMSCLW	54	149.7	2.167	0.049	2.118	41.6	208.0	8	16
10	BITPLW	58	147.9	0.033	0.0004	0.033	41.2	206.0	10	12
11	IITRLW	78	119.4	1.903	0.935	0.968	40.2	201.2	11	7
12	IITDLW	64	128.8	2.08	1.323	0.757	39.4	197.0	12	4
13	IIMALW	68	123.5	0.618	0.0417	0.577	38.5	192.7	13	21
14	IITGLW	64	126.6	0.032	0.0005	0.032	38.1	190.7	14	8
15	IISERKLW	38	146.6	2.178	0.793	1.384	37.8	189.0	15	22
16	IITHLW	43	141.1	2.043	0.976	1.068	37.6	188.2	16	19

17	NITTLW	51	132.7	2	1	1	37.5	187.7	17	11
18	IARILW	48	135.2	2	1	1	37.4	187.2	18	18
19	JNCASRLW	44	137.7	1.677	0.071	1.609	37.0	185.1	19	10
20	SINPLW	53	128.9	1.487	0.487	1	37.0	184.9	20	17
21	NITCLW	50	128.1	3.362	2.034	1.328	37.0	184.8	21	15
22	IITMLW	57	125.1	1.043	0.423	1.044	36.9	184.6	22	3
23	IIITHLW	39	141.5	0.008	0.0004	0.008	36.1	180.5	23	13
24	TIFRMLW	37	135.6	3.010	1.932	1.078	35.7	178.6	24	5
25	NITKLW	48	110.9	1.934	0.888	1.046	32.6	162.8	25	24

The ISB Hyderabad Library Website (187.5 score) scored first position in Web Analyzer Test Score Ranking followed by IIT Kanpur Library Website (161.6) at second position and NIT Rourkela Library Website (159) being at third position whereas last position was attained by NIT Karnataka Library Website obtaining 110.9 out of a total score of 260. The Mean, Median and Standard Deviation of Web Analyzer Test Score of library websites are 132.30, 125.1 and 26.40 respectively.

IISER Pune Library Website (9.182) scored first position in Web Impact Factor Ranking followed by NIT Calicut Library Website (3.3) which scored second position and Tata Institute of Fundamental Research, Mumbai Library Website (3.01) was at third position whereas the last position was scored by IIT Bombay Library Website (0.0003). Mean, Median and Standard Deviation of the Web Impact Factor score are 1.70, 1.5 and 1.26 respectively.

The IISER Pune Library Website (4.062) scored first position in the Revised Web Impact Factor Ranking followed by NIT Calicut Library Website (2.034) which scored second position and the Tata Institute of Fundamental Research, Mumbai Library Website (1.932) which scored third position whereas the last position was scored by IIT Bombay Library Website (0.0001). Mean, Median and Standard Deviation of the Revised Web Impact Factor are 0.47, 0.419 and 0.55 respectively.

The IISER Pune Library Website (5.119) scored first position in the Overall Web Impact Factor Ranking followed by The Institute of Mathematical Sciences Library Website (2.118) which scored second position and IISER Kolkata Library Website (1.38) that scored the third position whereas the last position was held by IIT Bombay Library Website (0.0001). The mean, median and standard deviation of the Overall Web Impact Factor was 1.23, 1.015 and 0.96 respectively.

To calculate the Composite Rank from the webometric techniques i.e. Web Indicators, Web Analyzer Test Score (WATS), Web Impact Factor, Revised Web Impact Factor and Overall Web Impact Factor were summed up and their Mean Score was calculated. The ISB Hyderabad Library Website (ISBHLW) scored first position in composite ranking of library websites with total score of 246.1 and mean score of 49.2 followed by IIT Kanpur Library Website (IITKLW) at second position with a total score of 230.9 and mean score of 46.2 followed by NIT Rourkela Library Website (NITRLW) which was at third position with a total score of 229.1 and mean score of 45.8. The last position was scored by NIT Karnataka Library Website (NITKLW) with total score of 162.8 and mean score of 32.6. It was also found that there is a difference in ranking of Institutional Websites and the ranking of Library Websites. This is because the Library Website is just a part of the Institutional Website which includes other aspects, for example Departments, Admissions, Alumani, Training and Placement, Research Output, etc.

Thus, it can be summarized that the library websites of most institutions have a long way to go before attaining some semblance of national standards leave alone international stands. Most of the institutional websites studied fared quite poorly on the large range of indicators in all five blocks. It is interesting to note that many of the apex institutions of higher education formed the basis for the current study.

These were a few among several others indicators. Once the institutions have upgraded themselves suitably on all the requisite indicators they would become at par with the international standards of structure and function of library websites the world over. Therefore, there is tremendous scope for further and diversified research on the topic.

The author has detailed the library websites' characteristics and presented their positioning through several methods of ranking established globally. These are discussed further in detail as well.

Thus, overall it can be seen that there are large gaps in the fulfillment of the essential pre requisites of websites, their structure and function. Much work needs to be done on all the websites that have been studied. This study has been a pioneering work which for the first time has pin pointed the lacunae in the library websites of various Research and Technical institutions. It also gives insights into how the websites that were lagging behind could be upgraded to a standardized Research and Technical library website.

5.3. STEPS FOR INCREASING VISIBILITY OF A LIBRARY WEBSITE

1. Each page of the library website should be linked to the homepage. Users should be directed to the required page through path information.
2. Library web pages should be downloaded faster. There should be avoidance of use of flash animation, background sounds, horizontal scrolling. The images should be moderate in size.
3. Web pages should be written in proper html based texts so that search engines are able to scroll the website easily and the overall visibility of the website increases. The web pages should have appropriate headings. Information provided on these web pages should be structured with improved user interface. Well designed web pages attract users. Well constructed web pages can be navigated easily, making quick and easy travel throughout the entire website (g.suit.google.com, n.d.).
4. The libraries should be involved in providing access to information through various quality web

indicators which should be user friendly. These indicators have user acceptance and usability and maximize the library website usage.

5. Links are arranged in various broader categories so that users can access the pages easily. Broken or duplicate links should be avoided. This will improve the rank of the library website. Link Management is an essential part of website maintenance.
6. The library website can be tested by Web Analyzer on regular intervals to check the status of those aspects of the website that cannot be evaluated through human eyes. A few effective Web Analyzers suggested here are Ahrefs, Sitebeam, Site Analyzer, GT Matrix, etc.
7. Design and content of the library website should be consistent i.e. heading size; font choice, coloring, button styles, spacing, design element, photo choice etc. should be in an optimized state. Everything should be themed to make the design coherent between pages and on the same page. Drastic design changes from one page to the other can lead users to feel lost and lose trust in the site.
8. Librarians should be given proper training regarding content strategy and evaluation processing of their library websites.
9. Automation software should be linked to the library website.
10. Approval for updating the library website process should be easy.
11. Required addons and extensions should be present in the library website.
12. Library websites should be operational on mobiles and tabs, saving the time of the user and also making it more user friendly in the latest IT environment.
13. The departmental (branch) library website should

be designed and maintained in such a way to fulfill subject specific information needs of the users in an appropriate way. The departmental library website should provide a link to the main (institutional) library website.

14. The library website is an integral part of the institutional website. The library website should include information about services and resources provided by the library and its related links. All aspects of the library should be covered. Quality content and design is the number one driver of search engine ranking. Regularly updating the library content improves the quality and rank of the library website. The date on which it is updated should be mentioned on the home page of the library website to facilitate the users.

5.4. FUTURE PROSPECTS

In view of the present research work further studies can also be beneficial. The book is confined only to the evaluation of 25 library websites of Research and Technical Institutes of India. There is still tremendous scope for further research. In addition, comparative studies can be undertaken to analyze the status of library websites of Indian Higher Educational Institutes and World Higher Educational Institutes. The library websites can also be evaluated through Web Content Accessibility Guidelines (WCAG) 2.1, Web Analyzers like Ahrefs, Sitebeam, Site Analyzer, GT Matrix, etc. Thus, the author presents vistas of research possibilities from which can emerge structured policy implications in the world of website efficiency all over the globe in general and within the country in particular.

References

Aguillo, I.F., Granadino, B., Ortega, J.L. & Prieto, J.A. (2006). Scientific research activity and communication measured with cybermetrics indicators. *Journal of the American Society for Information Science and Technology, 57*(10), 1296–1302. doi:10.1002/asi.20433

Almind, T.C. & Ingwersen, P. (1997). Informetric analyses on the world wide web: methodological approaches to 'webometrics'. *Journal of Documentation, 53*(4), 404-426. doi:10.1108/eum0000000007205

Arshas, A. & Ameen, K. (2015). Usage patterns of Punjab university library website: A transactional log analysis study. *The Electronic Library, 33*(1), 65–74. doi:10.1108/el-12-2012-0161

ARWU World University Rankings 2015/ Academic Ranking of World Universities (n.d). Retrieved October 28, 2017, from http://www.shanghairanking.com/

Babu, B.R., Narendra Kumar, A.M. & Gopala krishnan, S. (2009). Credibility of university websites in Tamil Nadu.*DESIDOC Journal of Library & Information Technology, 29*(3), 15–28. doi:10.14429/djlit.29.248.

Babu, B. R., Jeyshankar, R. & Rao, P. N. (2010). Websites of Central Universities in India: A Webometric Analysis. *DESIDOC Journal of Library & Information Technology, 30*(4), 33-43. doi:10.14429/djlit.30.458.

Babu, B.R., Narendra Kumar, A.M. & Gopalakrishnan, S. (2009). Credibility of university websites in Tamil Nadu.*DESIDOC Journal of Library & Information Technology, 29*(3), 15–28. doi:10.14429/djlit.29.248.

Baharum, A. & Jaafar, A. (2013). Users' Expectation of Web Objects Location: Case Study of ASEAN Countries. *Advances in Visual Informatics Lecture Notes in Computer Science,* 383-395. doi:10.1007/978-3-319-02958-0_35.

Basavaraj, S. (2017).*library websites of R and D institutions of Government of India: An evaluative study.* Gulbarga University.

BITS Pilani.(n.d.). Retrieved December 13, 2016, from http://www.bits-pilani.ac.in/

Bjorneborn, L. & Ingwersen, P. (2001).Perspectives of webometrics. *Scientometrics, 50*(1), 65-82.

Bjorneborn, L. & Ingwersen, P. (2004).Towards a basic framework for webometrics. *Journal of the American Society for Information Science and Technology, 55*(14), 1216-1227.

Brower, S.M., (2004). Academic health sciences library website navigation: an analysis of forty-one websites and their navigation tools. *Journal of the Medical Library Association, 92*(4),412-420.

Central Library IIT Bombay | Home. Retrieved December 19, 2016, from http:// *www.library.iitb.ac.in/*

Central Library - NITC.(n.d.). Retrieved July 20, 2016, from http://www.library.nitc.ac.in/

Central Library Indian Institute of Technology Bhubaneswar.(n.d.). Retrieved January 22, 2016, from http://library.iitbbs.ac.in/

Central Library, IIT Delhi. (n.d.). Retrieved September 1, 2016, from http://library.iitd.ac.in/

Central Library, IIT Kharagpur | I go into my library and all history unrolls before me - Alexander Smith. (n.d.). Retrieved March 12, 2016, from http://www.library.iitkgp.ernet.in/

Central Library, NITK: Homepage. (n.d.). Retrieved August 31, 2016, from http://library.nitk.ac.in

Chow, A.S., Bridges, M. & Commander, P. (2014). The Website Design and Usability of US Academic and Public Libraries. *Reference & User Services Quarterly, 53*(3), 253-265.

Databases - Indian Institute of Technology Hyderabad.(n.d.). Retrieved December 18, 2016, from http://www.bing.com/cr

Dragulanescu, N.G. (2002). Website quality evaluations: Criteria and tools. *International Information & Library Review, 34*(3), 247–254. doi:10.1080/10572317.2002.10762580

Elsayed, A. M. (2016). Web content strategy in higher education institutions: the case of King Abdulaziz University. *Information Development.* doi:10.1177/0266666916671387

Gangurde, M. (2017).*Evaluation of libraries website of selected management institutes of national and international repute.* North Mharashtra University.

Gharibeniazi, M., Kamran, M.K.A. & Gahaebi, A. (2015). Iranian State University Websites.*International Journal Science and Management. 13*(1),71-85.

Gsuite.google.com. (2017). *Gsuit : Collaboration & Productivity Apps for Business. (online).* Available at http://gsuit.google.com/ [Accessed 29 January 2017].

G. T. Matrix (2016). Website speed and performance optimization. Retrieved September 30, 2017, from https://gtmetrix.com/

IISER Kolkata - Library (n.d). Retrieved Februrary 14, 2016 www.iiserkol.ac.in/facility/library

IISER Pune Library (n.d.). Retrieved December 13, 2016 www.iiserpune.ac.in/~library/

Ingwersen, P. (1998). The calculation of web impact factors.*Journal of Documentation, 54*(2), 236-243. doi:10.1108/eum 0000000007167

Indian Agricultural Research Institute.(n.d.). Retrieved August 22, 2016, from http://iari.res.in

Indian Institute of Management, Ahmedabad - IIMA.(n.d.). Retrieved February 16, 2016, from https://web.iima.ac.in/

Indian School of Business (ISB) | Management Education.(n.d.). Retrieved November 3, 2016, from http://www.bing.com/ cr?

Iqbal, M. & Warraich, N.F. (2012). Usability evaluation of an academic library website: A case of the University of the Punjab. *Pakistan Journal of Library & Information Science,13,*1-11.

Islam, A., & Tsuji, K. (2011).Evaluation of Usage of University Websites in Bangladesh. *DESIDOC Journal of Library & Information Technology, 31*(6), 469-479. doi:10.14429/ djlit.31.6.1322

Islam, M.A. & Alam, M.S. (2011).Webometric study of private universities in Bangladesh.*Malaysian Journal of Library & Information Science, 16*(2), 115-126.

Jawaharlal Nehru Centre for Advanced Scientific Research. (n.d.). Retrieved June, 2016, from http://www.jncasr.ac.in/

Jalal, S.K. (2013). A Comparative Weblink Analysis among Top Indian, Asian and World Universities. *DESIDOC Journal of Library and Information Technology, 33(2),* 131-140.doi: 10.14429/djlit.33.2.4201.

Jalal, S.K., Biswas, S.C. & Mukhopadhyay, P. (2010). Web Presence of Select Asian Countries: A Webometric Study. *Collnet Journal of Scientometrics and Information Management,4*(2), 57-68. doi:10.1080/09737766.2010.10700893

Jalal, S.K., Biswas, S.C. & Mukhopadhyay, P. (2009).Bibliometrics to Webometrics. *Information Studies, 15*(1), 3-20.

Jalal, S.K., Biswas, S.C. &Mukhopadhyay, P. (2010). Web impact factor and link analysis of select Indian Universities. *Annals of Library and Information Studies, 57*(1), 109-121.

Jalal, S.K., Biswas, S.C. & Mukhopadhyay, P. (2010). Web-based ranking and link analysis of central universities in India: A Webometric Analysis. *Information Studies, 16*(1), 3-26.

Jeyashree, S. & Ravichandran, R. (2013).Perspective of webometric tools for web impact assessment studies: A review. *International Journal of Library Science,2*(2), 43-48. doi:10.5923/j.library.2013020.03

Jeyshankar, R. & Babu, B.R. (2009).Websites of universities in Tamil Nadu: a webometric study. *Annals of Library & Information Studies, 56*(2),2.

Jeyshankar, R. & Sujitha, I.M. (2014). Link analysis of Websites of Universities in Kerala: A Webometric study. *International Journal of Library and Information Studies, 4* (2), 062-071.

Jeyshankar, R., Babu, B.R. & Nageshwar, P.R. (2014).Websites of Indian institutes of Management(IIMs): A webometric study. *e-Library Science Research Journal, 2*(7), 001-008.

Jeyshankar, R., Sujitha, I.M. & Valarmathi. (2012). A Web Pages of ICMR institutes Websites: A Webometric analysis. *Global Advanced Research Journal of Library, Information and Archival Studies, 1*(1), 006-018.

Joicy, A.J. & Varghese, R.R. (2011).Websites of research and development Institutions in India: A webometric study. *International Journal of Digital Library Service, 1*(2), 090-104.

Kalra, J. & Verma, R.K. (2011). Evaluation Indicators of Library Websites of Select Research.*Annals of Library & Information*

Studies,52(2), 139-150.

Kaushik, A. (2015). An Evaluation of National Institutes of Technology (NITs) Library Websites.*DESIDOC Journal of Library and Information Technology, 35(3),* 223-234.doi: 10.14429/djlit.35.3.8546.

Konnur, P.V., Rajani, S. & Madhusudhan, M. (2010). Academic Library Websites in Bangalore City, India: An Evaluative Study. *Library Philosophy & Practice*, 1-14.

Kuchi T. (2006). Communicating mission: An analysis of academic library web sites. *Journal of Academic Librarianship* , *32*(2),148–154.

Lakshminath Bezbaroa Central Library - IIT Guwahati Retrieved December 13, 2016, from *https://www.iitg.ac.in/lib/*

Library | IIIT Hyderabad (n.d.) Retrieved November 2, 2016. https://oldwww.iiit.ac.in/institute/images/library.

Mahatma Gandhi Central Library, IIT Roorkee Retrieved December 3, 2016, from *mgcl.iitr.ac.in/*

Margam, M. & Prakash, S. (2013). Websites of Indian Institutes of Technology: A Webometric Study. *International Journal of Library and Information studies, 3*(4), 93-107.

Margam, M. & Shukla, S. (2012). Content evaluation of Indian Institutes of Technology Library Websites in India.World Digital Library, 5 (2), 001-020.

MHRD, National Institute Ranking Framework (NIRF). (2016). Retrieved September 30, 2016, from https://www.nirfindia.org/

Mierzecka, A. & Suminas, A. (2016). Academic library website functions in the context of users information needs. *Journal of Librarianship and Information Science*.doi:10.1177/0961000616664401

Mohammed, A., Garba, A., & Umar, H. (2016). University Library Websites in Nigeria: An Analysis of Content. *World Digital Libraries-An international journal, 9*(2), 121-130.

Murty, Y. (n.d.). IITM Central Library. Retrieved August 1, 2016, from http://www.cenlib.iitm.ac.in/

Nava Nalanda Central Library, Thapar University catalog.(n.d.). Retrieved May 24,2016

National Institute of Technology, Rourkela - Central Library.(n.d.). Retrieved January 4, 2016, from http://www.bing.com/cr

National Institute of Technology, Trichy.(n.d.). Retrieved October 13, 2016, from https://www.nitt.edu

Noruzi, A. (2005). Web impact factors for Iranian Universities. *Webology,2*(1), 11th ser. Retrieved from http://www.webology.ir/2005/v2n1/a11.html

Noruzi, A. (2006). The web impact factor: a critical review. *The Electronic Library, 24*(4), 490-500. doi:10.1108/02640470610689188

P K Kelkar Library, IIT Kanpur. (n.d.). Retrieved June 8, 2016, from http://pkklib.iitk.ac.in/

Prabakaran,R. & Lihitbar.(2015). Web Link Analysis and Web Impact Factor of Space Library Websites.10th International CALIBER, March12-14, 2015.

Ranking Web. (2016). Retrieved September 30, 2016, from http://www.webometrics.info/

Ranking. (n.d). Retrieved October 14, 2016 from https://www.timeshighereducation.com/world-university-ranking

Ramanayaka, K. H., Chen, X., & Shi, B. (2018).Application of Webometrics Techniques for Measuring and Evaluating Visibility of University Library Websites in Sri Lanka. *Journal of the University Librarians Association of Sri Lanka, 21*(1).

Salisbury, P. & Griffis, M. R. (2014). Academic library mission statements, web sites, and communicating purpose.*The Journal of Academic Librarianship, 40*(6), 592–596. doi:10.1016/j.acalib.2014.07.012

Shukla, A. & Tripathi, A. (2010). Establishing Content awareness evaluation criteria for library websites: A case study of Indian Academic Library Websites. *Annals of Library and Information Studies, 57,* 403-416.

Shukla, A. & Tripathi, A. (2015).*Webometric studies and libraries.* New Delhi: EssEss Publication.

Shukla, A. & Vanlalfeli. (2014). Webometric analyses of library websites of Indian Institutes of Technology.*Journal of Advacements in Library Sciences, 1*(2), 34-48.

Sitebeam | Test your websites for everything Retrieved December 15, 2016, from *https://sitebeam.net/*

Thelwall, M. (2000).Web Impact Factors and Search Engine coverage.*Journal of Documentation, 56*(2), 185–189. doi:10.1108/00220410010803801

Thelwall, M. (2009).*Introduction to Webometrics: Quantitative web research for the social sciences.* San Rafael, CA: Morgan Claypool Publishers, United States.

The Institute of Mathematical Sciences.(n.d.). Retrieved March 10,2016, from http://www.imsc.res.in/

TIFR Library E-Journals(n.d.). Retrieved July 2,2016 www.tifr.res.in/~sirc/ejournals%28E%29.html

Towards the global knowledge society- unesco. Retrieved September 30, 2016, from portal.unesco.org/education/en/files/7422/...doc/gf7_vandamme_document.doc

Varadharajalu, J., & Dhanavandan, S.(2017). Analysis of Web Impact Factor (WIF) for the Website of State Universities in Kerala.*International Journal of Library and Information Studies7(1)* .

Vasantha, R.N. & Harinarayana, N.S. (2008). An analysis of usability features of library websites. *Annals of Library and Information Studies,55*, 111-122.

Verma, M. K. & Devi, K. K. (2016). Web Content and Design Trends of Indian Institutes of Management (IIMs) Libraries Website: An Analysis. *DESIDOC Journal of Library & Information Technology, 36*(4), 220-227. doi:10.14429/djlit.36.4.9983

Verma, M. K. & Brahma, K. (2017).A Webometric analysis of select Non-Profit Organizations (NGOs) of Assam.*KIIT Journal of Library and Information Management,* 4 (1).

Verma, M. K. & Brahma, K. (2017). A webometric analysis of National Libraries' websites in South Asia. *Annals of Library and Information Studies (ALIS), 64*(2), 116-124.

Verma, M. K. & Brahma, K. (2017). Websites of Central Universities in North East India: A Webometric Analysis. *DESIDOC Journal of Library & Information Technology, 37(3),* 186-191. doi:10.14429/djlit.37.3.10906.

Verma, M. K. & Devi, K. K. (2015). Content Analysis of Central Universities Library Websites of North Eastern States of India: A Survey. *Journal of Research in Librarianship, 2*(5), 48-59.

Vijayakumar, M. (2012). Webometric Analysis of Web Presence and Links of SAARC Countries.*DJLIT DESIDOC Journal of Library & Information Technology,32*(1), 70-76. doi:10.14429/djlit.32.1.1409

Walia, P.K. & Gupta, M. (2012). Web Impact Factor of Select National

Libraries' Websites. *DESIDOC Journal of Library & Information Technology, 32*(4), 347-352. doi:10.14429/djlit.32.4.2530

Walia, P.K. & Gupta, M. (2013). Usability analysis of Homepage of Websites of National Libraries in Asia.*Library Philosophy & Practice*, 1-20.

Walia, P.K. & Kaur, P. (2010). Government of India Websites: A Study. *DESIDOC Journal of Library & Information Technology, 30*(4), 3-10. doi:10.14429/djlit.30.454

Walia, P.K. & Gupta, M. (2012). Web Impact Factor of Select National Libraries' Websites. *DESIDOC Journal of Library & Information Technology,32*(4), 347-352. doi:10.14429/djlit.32.4.2530

Web Analytics Definitions - Digital Analytics Association.(2007). Retrieved from September 20, 2016, http://www.digitalanalyticsassociation.org/Files/PDF.../WebAnalytics DefinitionsVol1.pdf.

West Bengal Public Library Network.(n.d.). Retrieved November 3, 2016, from http://www.bing.com/cr?

Wijayaratne, A.L. & Singh, D. (2015). Developing an academic library website model, a designer's checklist, and an evaluative instrument.*Electronic Library, 33*(1), 35-51. doi:10.1108/EL-11-2012-0115

Wilson, D.E. (2015). Web content and design trends of Alabama academic libraries.*Electronic Library, 33*(1), 88-102. doi:10.1108/EL-05-2013-0100

World University Rankings. (2016). Retrieved September 28, 2016, from https://www.timeshighereducation.com/world-university-rankings/2016/world-ranking